THE ESSENTIALS OF COUNSELLING AND PSYCHOTHERAPY IN PRIMARY SCHOOLS

Dear Pen,
For the times we've
shared & beyond...
Love
Shelley

THE ESSENTIALS OF COUNSELLING AND PSYCHOTHERAPY IN PRIMARY SCHOOLS

On Being a Specialist Mental Health Lead in Schools

Gary Winship and Shelley G. MacDonald

Routledge
Taylor & Francis Group

LONDON AND NEW YORK

First published 2018
by Routledge
2 Park Square, Milton Park, Abingdon, Oxon OX14 4RN

and by Routledge
711 Third Avenue, New York, NY 10017

Routledge is an imprint of the Taylor & Francis Group, an informa business

British Library Cataloguing in Publication Data

A C.I.P. for this book is available from the British Library

ISBN-13: 978-1-78220-047-5 (pbk)

Typeset in Palatino LT Std
by Medlar Publishing Solutions Pvt Ltd, India

Printed and bound by CPI Group (UK) Ltd, Croydon, CR0 4YY

Dedicated to
Logie, Lewis, and Bonnie

CONTENTS

ACKNOWLEDGEMENTS

To the many primary school staff who have been united in their dedication to making better tomorrows for their pupils, and the children and their parents who have provided the inspiration for this book. Pippa Weisz and UKCP book series editorial board. Colleagues and students involved with the MA Counselling Children and Young People course at University of Nottingham; Max Biddulph, Belinda Harris, Lindsay Cooper, David Murphy, Stephen Joseph, and Jenny Good-fellow-Pemsell. Many others whose work and practice is gratefully acknowledged; Sibell Ali, Penny Askew, Julie Chantrey, Sunny Chohan, Carolyn Grundy, Barbara Hopton, Stephen Jon, Maya Mamish, Stacey Parkes, Hannah Saxton, Karrin White. Colleagues who have been working on research looking at school age school suicides and self-harm, especially; Marie Armstrong, Nigel Chapman, Dilip Nathan, and Ellen Townsend. Peter Wilson, Harry Ferguson, Bob Hinshelwood, John Diamond, Steve Briggs, and Al Stokeld, have been valuable sources of practice guidance. Others who we know who are working with children and young people in Nottingham as part of a collective effort of early intervention; Roger Henry, Melitta Bryan, and Graham Allen (MP), all of whom have shaped and influenced the perspectives shared in this book. Where ideas in this book meet with approval we acknowledge the collective influence of many friends and colleagues, for any short-comings and errors we take full responsibility.

ABOUT THE AUTHORS

Gary Winship (PhD, MA, Dip GP Psych, UKCP registered Psycho-analytic Psychotherapist, NMC Registered), associate professor at the School of Education in Nottingham, course leader MA Trauma Studies. He has taught and trained many students from a number of countries including South Korea, Taiwan, UK, Belize, Tahiti, Belgium, Greece, Turkey, China, Saudi Arabia, and Syria among others. A senior fellow of the Institute of Mental Health, Nottingham University. Formerly lecturer at the University of Sheffield (2004–2006), University of Reading (2000–2004), and visiting lecturer at University College London (UCL), University of Greenwich, University of East London (UEL), and Goldsmiths, University of London. Also, senior adult psychotherapist at Berkshire NHS Trust, Broadmoor and Maudsley Hospitals. In 2011 he was invited to deliver a keynote address at the twenty-second China Congress for the Mental Health of Children, held in Ningbo, China where he talked about his research into birth order and only children. He has published over ninety clinical papers and six books. His website: www.winship.info has had more than eight million hits in the last ten years. He has led a number of research projects including; psychosocial aspects of malicious fire starting (ESRC, 2004–2007); therapeutic use of clay with children and adolescents (2011–2012) and school age suicide and self-harm (2012–). An article in *The Times* (2010) described Gary as one of the two leading experts in the UK on the psychology of fire starting.

Shelley G. MacDonald (MA [Tavistock/UEL], MA [Glasgow], BACP Accredited) Shelley is a counselling psychotherapist with twenty-five years of experience working in frontline services with children and young people, in residential social services and schools. She managed primary schools counselling and psychotherapy services and is currently head of counselling with Leicester Women's Counselling Centre.

FOREWORD

Peter Wilson

At the heart of this book is a strong and compelling plea that we should all take notice, ever more so than in the past, of the experience and plight of primary school aged children and counsellors/psychotherapists—two groups of people, quite different yet at times closely involved with each other. Children obviously matter not least because of their vitality and abundant potential but also because of their vulnerability to mal-treatment and neglect. Counsellors and psychotherapists matter too, though so often misunderstood and marginalised. The authors, Gary Winship and Shelley MacDonald have written here an impassioned book, a bold and forceful account of the mental harm inflicted upon children and of the challenges of practicing counselling and psycho-therapy. What does it take to "make" a healthy and happy child? What components, elements, influences, pressures are at stake?

The chapter headings in the book show clearly the course of the authors' thinking about the essential areas to be covered—on schooling, on noticing, on relating, on knowing, on curiosity and protecting. So much is included in these chapters that we are left in no doubt about the complexity of primary school life and of the task of the counsellor/psychotherapist in it. The school for example is not simply seen as a place in which children come to learn the three R's. In this book, it is seen much more as a place of social and emotional learning—so much so that the authors have no hesitancy in seeing it functioning as a therapeutic community. Many of course, may well blanch at this, to be told that they have to have that word "therapy" dragged into the province of a school. School, they will insist is solely about education, not therapy; "teachers are not therapists, thank you very much".

And yet we know full well that the primary school is the first new world into which children delve beyond the familiarity of their families. It is where they encounter other people from other families and cultures. It is where they bump into other children of their own age and discover the collisions of differences and delights of similarities. It is where they experience new kinds of conflicts and tensions both within themselves and between others. It is, in other words, a place where so much goes on other than the academic process of learning facts. The old arguments about the difference between what is considered to be education and what is considered to be health become superfluous.

There has been increasing recognition in recent years of the concept of the "whole school policy" in which all the many facets of school life are brought together in the interests of cultivating the full minds of children. To accomplish this a great deal of skill and competence is necessarily required. Clear authoritative leadership, effective governance and management, emotional and supervisory support for teachers, inclusion of parents, employment of counsellors/psychotherapists and above all a vision close to that of a a therapeutic community—all these are the essential ingredients in the grand mixture of school life.

Into the midst of all this steps the school counsellor/psychotherapist, at first sight something of a foreigner, arriving as he or she does with a different professional history and training from most of those who work in the school. How does she fit in? Is he welcomed? Or do there prevail varying degrees of resistance, the school counsellor/psychotherapist being seen as a nuisance or a luxury to be tolerated and maybe cast aside to the sidelines of school life, left to see a small number of individual children well out of view? Such a fate is not uncommon but certainly not to be countenanced in this book. On the contrary, the very thrust of the authors' argument is that the school counsellor/psychotherapist needs to establish herself as a very active and visible individual in the school—and it is with this emphasis on the counsellor/psychotherapist taking on a forthright and central position that the authors are introducing the essence of the "new" ingredients. This is in many respects a departure from the received wisdom of many other writers in the field who encourage taking a relatively low profile in the school and who urge caution in their practice and dealings with school staff, recommending discrete and limited involvement with teachers and others in the school.

It would be of course misleading to suggest that Winship and MacDonald are favouring the abandonment of established principles and ethics of counselling and psychotherapeutic practice. However, they are proposing that the counsellor/psychotherapist become more venturesome in their professional approach. In their opinion, the school counsellor/psychotherapist should be a lively presence in the school, working closely with teachers, parents, support workers, and with those in the wider network outside the school. Similarly, in his counselling work with individual or groups of children, the school counsellor/ psychotherapist should feel free to be more openly curious, pursuing lines of enquiry with the child, rather than always waiting for the child to come to express her thoughts in their own time. Equally, he should feel less afraid to interpret the meaning of some of their children's feelings and behaviours (that is to say, to make "educated guesses that take the form of questions")—rather than hold back for fear of being too intrusive or "analytical". As the authors so forcefully put it: "Psychotherapy as a politically mute psychic retreat can no longer be defended".

The clinical illustrations in this book are remarkable for their variety. In some cases, the counsellor/psychotherapist is practical, giving advice to parents and teachers and showing a readiness when necessary to meet a child where she is at, for example sitting alongside a child in his classroom. In other cases, the counsellor/psychotherapist is carrying out highly sophisticated and complicated psychotherapy with some seriously disturbed children and their parents. The authors show a willingness to look beyond the psychiatric diagnosis of these children, whether it be ADHD, autism or some other "disorder"; and to face and work through much of the emotional pain and fear which so many of the children suffer from. This work, carried out in weekly sessions, is without doubt, time and energy consuming. There is no illusion here of a quick fix or a magical cure and it is this honesty that makes so many of the clinical accounts in the book so credible.

It may come as something of a surprise to professionals working in the field that many people in the wider public still find it difficult to believe that children in primary school need counseling at all. Still, the old clichés tumble out—that children are "innocent", too "young to know" anything "better" and "best seen and not heard". By contrast, the authors of this book have a deep appreciation of the developmental difficulties that children face particularly in slowly finding out the nature of who they are and differentiating themselves from the claims or rejections of their parents. They also have a sharp insight into the many sensitivities and perceptions that children of this age possess—whether it be their awareness of each other, or their parents emotional preoccupations, or the tensions inherent in domestic violence or even in the emotional strain for the teachers who are teaching them.

What adds so much weight to this book is its well informed grounding in political awareness and conceptual understanding. The authors are very aware of the wide range of governmental policies in health and social services and in education that bear upon the every day life of schools. They also take great care in explaining the history and formulation of key concepts such as attachment, containment, transference, and counter transference, without which the practice of the counsellor/psychotherapist loses direction and focus.

Gary Winship and Shelley Macdonald give us a great deal to digest in this book. Truly, many ingredients making much good food for thought.

PREFACE

Emotional labour

It is an uncomfortable truth that there is a need for the provision of therapy for children and young people. We would wish that it were not so. Services like Childline and the Samaritans offer an indispensable listening ear at a point of crisis but sometimes there needs to be something more sustained, especially in cases where children and young people present with complex problems, for instance, those who come onto the radar of social services. School counsellors and psychotherapists are on the frontline and are therefore faced with the responsibility of bearing sustained witness to the distress that some children face.

The school psychotherapist can hold on to the child's story as it unfolds across months and sometimes years. At best, the psychotherapist who works with a child in a school might even shape their story. It is emotional labour if you will, though not in the sense of the therapist behaving with the formal pleasantries as in Hochschild's (1983) original concept in her book *The Managed Heart*, but rather the school psychotherapist works with a heavy heart. We consider emotional labour in the sense that Pam Smith (2011) so eloquently describes as the tough mental challenge of caring for people in need, where the positive impact of holding people in mind and the capacity to modulate one's emotional response to a client, particularly in an adverse interpersonal encounter, is a considerable practice asset. In the first place we need to understand the context of emotional labour, so in the first chapter we talk about "On schooling" and consider how a primary school can act as what we know to be a "therapeutic community". The school as a therapeutic community is our first essential ingredient; in a therapeutic community the aspiration is to create an environment where everyone can experience a sense of being cared for, where values are driven by the goal of sustaining and containing creative milieu and there is an atmosphere of transitional homeliness.

In the second chapter, "On noticing", we look at the core dimensions of observation, and consider the range of practitioner capabilities which lie at the heart of effective practice. The essentials of "noticing" encompasses a range of intuitions and skills, starting with the challenge of visual engagement. We consider the task of undertaking observation as preparation for the practice of psychotherapy in schools and look at examples of depth observation, not just seeing the surface of behaviour, but how to read the characteristics of emotion. We make a case that observation should also be the underpinning for honing and developing new conceptions about child development.

In the third chapter "On relating", we begin to develop some fundamental principles of relationship building and the formative stages of attachment and working with the client's sense of belonging, or lack of it. The idea of building a therapeutic alliance with the young client is seen as an essential ingredient that is the prerequisite to all that takes place in therapy thereafter. The idea of attachment and belonging, sits alongside the emotional task of "containment". In Chapter four "On knowing", we illustrate how the active mental process of thinking about the client and holding their emotional distress in mind has become one of the most valuable ideas in the practice of psychotherapy today. Containment in this sense is taken to be a psychological event, a task of holding in mind. But we also consider the way in which containment can be part of the fabric of the space where therapy takes place, the bricks and mortar of the building, the school and classroom spaces which we come to know as "containing spaces".

In Chapter Five we look at "curiosity" and consider how the therapist can develop their capacity and confidence to find out more about the client, without being unnecessarily intrusive. We tackle what seems to have become a taboo among many branches of counselling and psychotherapy, the question of asking questions. We assert that the therapist's curiosity is an essential ingredient and that it is necessary therein to ask questions. In attempting to develop an approach that we would see as having value across a range of therapeutic denominations, we demystify the psychoanalytic interpretative technique and show how imagination and free thinking are the necessary states of mind in the therapist which will engender the most conducive atmosphere for dialogue and progress in working with young clients.

In the final chapter we talk about "protecting" and look at the new frameworks for safeguarding in schools and in the lives of young children. We look at what we call the "safeguarding matrix", that is to say the social and cultural network of the child's world, alongside the life of the local community, which the therapist needs to hold in mind. The school itself is central to looking after the best interests of the child and we argue that the overarching framework for "protecting" is a new essential ingredient in the practice of the school psychotherapist.

Words for early intervention

Primarily, we are concerned in describing the role of talking therapy with young children. That is not to understate the importance of play and the role of creative therapeutic engagement, especially working psychotherapeutically with very young children, but we have set ourselves the task of looking more closely at play in another book, so rather the concept of play is conspicuous by its absence in this book. Finding the role of words is what concerns us here in the first place. We see words as food for thought, they wrap around feelings and when spoken out loud they can travel across the space between people making emotional connections possible. Valuing words in the process of talking therapy is hardly new, it is where the profession of psychotherapy began and even when the therapist is using creative materials like paint and clay, the process of finding words is still essential. But also there will be times when psychotherapists working with young, often traumatised children, will need to listen to silence. The psychotherapist must make sense of sounds, of pauses and stuttering, where language is inchoate.

Some colleagues, particularly Lacanians, argue that the unconscious is structured like a language in that it involves ciphering and deciphering. Words are well known to us long before we are born. We hear words before we see anything. Words are proto-mental, they form the first imprints of experience, and are as bodily as all of our other senses. In utero, baby will begin to have auditory sensations and in ordinary circumstances these experiences will be accompanied by sounds and words from mother, father and sometimes siblings. When all goes well, baby will learn that words can soothe and affirm, but also that words can be harsh, sometimes filled with hostility. Words can express hope and optimism, love and care, but they can also express wounds, full of hurt and despair. Words can tell the truth, but they can also hide it. Throughout this book, we position it is necessary for therapists to learn the dark side of the word and the emotional states that words seek to convey. For instance, love may be the older sibling of hate, but learning to sit with hate is a necessary attribute for the psychotherapist. Winnicott (1949) aptly referred to; "Hate in the countertransference". Too many therapists seem unwilling and incapable of sitting with hate, either their client's hate, or their own. Such difficult states of mind for the therapist are the crux of the work. Reassuring words are easy "gifts" in therapy, but children and young people have an uncanny knack of cutting through these.

What we hope to convey is the reality of how difficult it is to work with children and young people. By offering a combination of case reflections, evidence and theory, the aim is to provide the reader with information that is thought provoking, critically real as well as usefully practical. In turn we hope this will help the reader, who incidentally we would include teachers, nurses, doctors, social workers, psychologists, and parents, to feel more confident in their understanding of how to engage with children in distress. Some of the topics we cover in the book are demanding, but we speak as openly as we can. Most experienced counsellors and psychotherapists know that therapeutic change is wrung from engaging with conflict, bearing and then containing the pain before helping the client find a new synthesis for getting on in the world. Melanie Klein said as much as fifty per cent of the work is done in the negative transference. The therapist must be prepared to be the enemy if they are to help the child mount a campaign to triumph over the internal and external difficulties in their lives. Too many therapists just want to be the client's friend, but that's not enough. For many young people the world is a bleak place and that is where the therapist must tread.

We are looking at a storm of statistics on the current vulnerability of children and young people in Britain today; self-harm, suicide, mental health problems, drug and alcohol use, sexual abuse, female genital mutilation, trafficking, and radicalisation. At the time of writing police in Scotland are having to process thirty million illegal images of children being abused. We live and work post-Climbie, Baby P, Little Ted's Nursery in Plymouth, child sexual exploitation in Rochdale, the offences carried out by Jimmy Saville to name a few recent cases which have come to public light. Counsellors and psychotherapists need to embrace the statutory territory of child protection and safeguarding, even if they are working in private practice. Social Care thresholds are rising with the recession as fast as benefits are plummeting, and more cuts are on the horizon. Increasingly, counsellors and psychotherapists are in the frontline of early intervention, and this is no more so than in school mental health service provision. Child and Adolescent Mental Health Services (CAMHS) are overwhelmed and for the most part, only offer six to eight week interventions. The Any Qualified Provider (AQP) delivery of mental health services graft market governance onto human exchange and Paid by Outcomes (PbO) services mostly prioritise brief Cognitive Behavioural Therapies (CBT) which can too often fail to get to grips with the emotional and relational challenge of working with younger clients. It is into these gaps in service provision that the profession of counselling and psychotherapy should focus its ambitions and should speak up and speak out for early intervention.

Cornerstones

The updated version of *Working Together to Safeguard Children* (DfCSF, 2015) insists that all professionals collaborate where there are concerns around the physical and emotional wellbeing of a child. All the Serious Case Reviews (SCRs) we have looked at point to the necessity of working collaboratively between professionals if agencies are to provide an adequate safety net around the falling child. We need to consider the practice of psychotherapy with the provision of a collective model of public mental health. Models of progressive psychotherapy, particularly in the trajectory of psychotherapy with children and young people in the UK, emerge from the diaspora of European psychoanalysis with strong collectivist interpersonal interest. Post-Freudian, and especially Anna Freud and Melanie Klein, provide a key theoretical backcloth here. In distinction to North America where psychological therapies have a much stronger leaning towards positivist rather than critical approaches, the old European intellectual traditions have shaped a particularity of counselling and psychotherapy with an emphasis on models of conflict resolution. Whereas American psychologies have emphasised an ego-centred self-psychology, carved from an individualistic tradition of cultural reproduction, the European tradition is fashioned from a stronger connection to matters of the social mind.

We begin with the collectivist assertion that many young clients who present for therapy have experienced unhappiness or neglect where deprivation has been an underpinning factor. Most of the case studies in this book have been hewn from practices in geographical areas of significant social and cultural deprivation. From children and young people who have internalised a denigrated sense of self to those who drag themselves into the consulting room as if somehow it's their own fault. The work of counselling and psychotherapy described in this book should therefore be considered as events that are fundamentally political. One must remember that the children whose stories are heard in this book are children who were often poorly parented first and foremost by the state. There is an old African saying; "It takes a village to raise a child" and if we want our cities to raise children then we need a holistic approach where the professional "village" surrounding the child is thoroughly knitted, where inequalities are tackled by the rigorous best efforts to redistribute wealth.

Investing in parents in need must be a key agenda. When working with young children in particular engaging the parent is critical to therapeutic outcome. The child in therapy often gives voice to family disturbance. R. D. Laing tells us that it is useful to consider the family (and the broader society) as the source of mental health difficulties. He argued that; "the person who gets diagnosed is part of a wider network of extremely disturbed and disturbing patterns of communication" (Laing, 1984, p. 94). Furthermore, what we understand by "family" today is one of many shifting sands of social construction. Families can be complex, sometimes without one or other parent, sometimes headed by a grandparent or by two mothers or fathers. There are more blended families than ever before where divorced parents and step siblings come together, or where a single mother may have children from multiple fathers, or fathers who have multiple partners who have mothered their children. As such families may feel, at times, rather more churned than blended. We want to stress then that we see the children who present for psychotherapy as transgenerational emissaries for their families, their parents, siblings, grandparents and even for the neighbourhood where they live.

Furthermore, just as many in the public schooling system are groomed to move into positions of power, compliant with expectation, so too can children from socially deprived estates be readied unwittingly for the pathways available to them. A seven-year-old girl came to a session recently and brought with her a long history of poor school attendance. She was struggling to keep up in class. She said to her therapist; "I'm stupid, I can't read or write and I'm not clever. My brother said I won't be able to get a job and that I will always be poor". Is our response to say to this child that she is clever and she will get a job if she tries really hard and believes in herself? Do we blame her mother for not getting her to attend school more regularly and applaud a system which will fine her (and the family) for her failure? The therapist must do neither. Instead it is the first challenge to bear the emotion of a child who already feels defeated by her circumstances, then it is the patient task of building a therapeutic alliance, a quality relational exchange that will give the child an experience of being valued. Finally, the therapist must sustain engagement where the client can experience some new synthesis of a relationship where confidence and worth can flourish, with growing hope that life can be better.

Joined up eco-systems

Counsellors and psychotherapist are now compelled to work as part of a joined up system of health provision that stretches a common agenda across a number of professions. There are many parents who seek a medical diagnosis for their children, but equally, there are parents who feel patronised and disempowered by professionals. A diagnosis has all manner of constraints attached, but it may be a relief too, and it may release resources. For instance a diagnosis of high functioning autism can lead a parent to say; "I used to think he was just being difficult but now I understand he can't do it so I just work around it". But a diagnosis can become an altogether more radical and convincing idea to explore if we consider causal pathways. To that effect counsellors and therapists need to embrace the concept of shared diagnostics and the shared language of inter-professional working, and in doing so it is feasible to begin to reframe the biological territory that paediatricians and psychiatrists often inhabit. A good deal of the push towards a mental health agenda in schools (DfE, 2014) helpfully reconfigures our understanding of "behaviour" in terms of the social reasons for the behaviour. What we previously may have thought of as "bad behaviour", we now can re-cast as a communication pertaining to the child's difficulties and distress.

While we are being mindful of the here and now of the client in the therapy room, we need to think about the world of the client beyond the walls of the school. Who is looking out for these children as they roam their estates and neighbourhoods looking for experience beyond the family? Sometimes neighbourhoods are policed by gangs who are headed up by young people who belong to the most notorious family on the estate. Membership has to be measured up by a young person as they calculate whether it's better to be vulnerable to attack or join the gang who might deliver the attack and secure protection. The philosopher Zygmunt Bauman (2001) in his book *Community—Seeking Safety in an Insecure World*, tells us that we need to struggle to reconcile the tension that exists between freedom and security. Young people might need to lay some claim to the streets, to have a sense of freedom and ownership, and yet they need also to be held in the gaze of responsible others. The time when it was mostly parents who did this surveillance has long gone. The crisis is the absence of paternal gaze especially, and technology in the form of mobile phone connectivity, closed circuit television, social media, web records and so forth offers a virtual level of scrutiny, but there is something missing.

We need to consider neighbourhoods and their architecture because it shapes the minds of children. We might think about the psychological stressors in economic and ecological terms for example in urban environments; pollution, noise, population density, crime and so forth (Halpern, 1995). Strategies for "curing" ailing communities must include environmental planning as a means to "preventing" mental illness and in the compassionate design of communities, the primary school psychotherapist should seek to create the therapeutic spaces for those who might otherwise feel most marginalised. Government and local government can do much to rejuvenate ailing ghettos and fraying school buildings. Recreating spaces designed for social engagement such as skateparks, youth centres, urban allotments, basketball courts or football pitches, can give children pride in their environment and, by proxy, pride in themselves. But there is still so much more that could be done. Children are adept, only so far, at working out the moralities of the different spaces they inhabit. Left too much to their own devices they can bump into trouble around the streets of their estate and neighbourhood. Often these children will bring their lives into school the next day seeking out a different moral governance. Schools' core opening hours might be 8.00–4.00 but their reach is way beyond this. The school psychotherapist might do well to hold in mind the wider network of the community that presents in the session with the client.

The other horizon that this book focuses on is the need to think about the multicultural client base and the disproportionate number of white female, middle-aged counsellors in the profession of counselling and psychotherapy. How do we navigate the territorially contested waters of difference whilst the profession remains obstinately the same? If we do not share a culture with our clients we need to notice the differential in the room. We need to notice racism and its impact on mental health. Black boys, in particular, if things continue as they are now, will grow up more likely to be diagnosed with a serious mental health problem, more likely to be detained under the Mental Health Act, and for longer, and subject to heavier doses of medication than their white counterparts (Samuels, 2015). Are black boys less likely to be referred for therapy and to what extent do we see it as our responsibility as early intervention practitioners to secure a client base broadly representative of the diversity of the catchment we serve? To say we as practitioners don't notice the difference, that we treat all clients equally, must warrant further scrutiny.

Of late we have seen some disenfranchised men, some barely left youth, who have attacked those with a greater sense of belonging enjoying a concert at Manchester or the festivities of Bastille Day, a bite to eat in Munich, a night out in Orlando, a shopping trip in Baghdad, a gig in Paris. It is arguable that the less factional we are psychologically, locally, and globally the less likely we are to wage war, the more likely we are to develop a maturing psyche not poised on the brink of a schizoid standoff. The school counsellor and psychotherapist situated in an early intervention setting such as a primary school is uniquely positioned to try to offer up something healing to the dislocated, marginal child. Creating better tomorrows for one child can create stable tomorrows for the many.

Who is this book for?

In short, this book has ideas for everyone and we encourage colleagues and students to develop a plural knowledge base that is not shackled to one modality. The primary care mental health agenda is now one that embraces a complex interweave of presenting client disorders and difficulties. Many conditions are now considered in composite terms rather than as isolated illnesses that have linear solutions. The rubric of dual and multiple diagnosis has been helpful in conveying the complexity of presentation. In other words, the singularity of defining an illness has been replaced by a way of thinking that acknowledges the reality that there are number of intersecting issues that the client brings to therapy. Arguably, counselling and psychotherapy approaches should be flexible to meet these complex challenges, and approaches should not be defined in terms of the singular denomination of the practitioner. Rather the reflexive skills of the practitioner should be drawing on a range of knowledge bases, which inform us about the array of current challenges presented by clients.

Most counselling and psychotherapy trainings focus practitioner preparation efforts in the direction of experiential learning, with a curriculum that promotes an environment of learning that emphasises personal development experiences from which the practitioner can learn about themselves, with opportunities to develop their own inventories of strengths and weaknesses, blind spots and learning edges. Students are often looking for tricks and tactics and might find it frustrating that they are encouraged to self-discover. With the emphasis on experiential learning in training, the role of this book is to provide a bridge between theory and practice. There should be no doubt that we see this book sitting alongside practice development and practitioner preparation fortified by experiencing a good enough personal therapy for ourselves. That is, if we have not placed ourselves in the hands of a professional, how can we genuinely ask it of others in our care?

If you are considering a career in counselling and psychotherapy with children and young people, or have recently qualified, you might be reflecting on what sort of person you are becoming, and will become. Will you be of sound enough mind, or had enough therapy to justify that you are capable enough to work with a young person who feels at odds with the world around them? Can you work under pressure and think on your feet? Do you have the sort of intuitive mind that will help you find the right words when words otherwise seem to fail? Are you creative and able to demonstrate enough freedom of expression in your own enterprise to know that you might be able to help someone else find their own creativity? Can you bear criticism, even if it might have nothing to do with you? Can you manage your own negative feelings, withstand your own foibles, say the wrong thing and still know you are driven by compassion? Can you accept that you have blind spots, even though you can't see them and that you can sit with ease in your own skin even when it starts to creep? And can you hold your nerve to listen, when all around you have lost theirs?

If your answer these questions is an emphatic "yes", then working with disturbed children and young people is not for you; you should read no further, because surety is not a virtue of a good enough thera-pist. If the answer to these questions is "no", then you should protect yourself and find a job that doesn't bring a weight of heavy emotional baggage that might break your own wellbeing. However, if the answer to the foregoing questions is either; "maybe" or especially "I hope so", then perhaps you should read on. The job of working with young clients is for those who can sit with doubt and uncertainty and treat them equally as allies. If you can recognise the privilege of working with a young client who today might feel like the world is caving in, but who tomorrow might achieve great things, then you might well become the therapist that you need to be.

CHAPTER ONE

On schooling—a therapeutic community approach

Brief

In this chapter we argue that a whole school approach to mental health wellbeing can be framed by adapting a "therapeutic community" approach drawing on the established principles of working therapeutically with children and young people (Diamond, 2016). A therapeutic community ideology is positioned as an opportunity to think more expansively about mental health in primary schools, envisaging a model where all parts of the school can work together to create a milieu conducive to wellbeing. In this system based approach, we envisage the role of the school psychotherapist as a facilitator who can hold in mind the identified client within the context of an array of dynamic interactions throughout the life of a school. That is to say, while concentrating on the focal time spent with the young clients, either individually or in a group situation, school psychotherapists should also pay heed to the overall context of the school as a psychologically informed therapeutic environment. In a broad sense we need to position the concept of the school, any school, as an adapted therapeutic community with the school counsellor or psychotherapist as a facilitator who fosters a culture that we might consider in terms of a whole school approach to sustaining a therapeutic milieu.

Mental Health & Behaviour in Schools (DfE, 2014/2015) emphasised "key" presenting areas such as substance misuse, self-harm, eating disorders, and attachment disorders and recommends evidenced based approaches, particularly cognitive behavioural and psychoanalytic therapies. The report *Mental Health & Behaviour in Schools* report follows emerging research that school-based counselling and psychotherapy is effective (Daniunaite, Cooper, & Forster, 2015). Broadly speaking there are two types of school counsellor, one is parachuted in from outside only seeing individual children intermittently for one-to-one therapy and the other is the therapist who is in situ. In the case of the in situ approach, the therapist has the opportunity to embed themselves in the community of the school. The in situ therapist typically has a dedicated office and therapy room, and is seen as an integral part of the school team. They are able to avail themselves of opportunities to observe children in class and at play. They come to understand the competing demands of running a school (and in the case of Academies, running a business), and they are able to grasp the trials and tribulations of the teachers' lives from close hand. Further, they get an opportunity to work with parents and, in turn, they come to understand the broader community where the school is situated. When there is an embedded counselling service, a self-referral drop-in provision can be offered so all the children can access a counsellor if needed. This model offers scope for the school counsellor to be invited to attend CAF's (Common Assessment Framework) and other multi-agency meetings. And whilst the peripatetic counsellor is afforded an outsider's objectivity, an experienced school counsellor should be able to maintain the necessary distance to hold an overview of the complex interplay of dynamics that exert influence in any school. It with this type of model in mind that we develop the idea of a whole school therapeutic community approach.

Policy and practice overview

This chapter considers the raft of policy changes and practices in recent years that have altered the landscape of early intervention and the mental health agenda in primary schools. Other recent initiatives include the evolution of initial teacher training focusing on attachment based approaches to furthering teacher's understanding of child development.

The comprehensive review of Initial Teacher Training (ITT) which was carried out by Sir Andrew Carter and published in January 2015 made key recommendations that all ITT should include a purposeful grounding in the theory of child and adolescent emotional development with an emphasis on attachment theory. The Carter Review also concluded that there should be accredited training in attachment based practice for all staff working in schools. The Government's response to the Carter Review has seen the Secretary of State for Education establish a sector task force to identify a framework of Core ITT content. However, with the recent Brexit vote still reverberating around Westminster, with the installation of a new Prime Minister and a radically reshaped cabinet, it remains to be seen how these policy initiatives will unfold. Suffice to say that much of the legislation protecting and extending children's rights comes from the European Union.

A cross party House of Commons Health Committee Report (HC 342, 2014) *Children's and Adolescents' Mental Health and CAMHS* recognised the crisis of service provision and concluded that schools needed to do more to fill in the gaps left by the shortfall of CAMHS resources, recommending that the DfE do the following:

> Look to include a mandatory module on mental health in initial teacher training, and include mental health modules as part of ongoing professional development in schools for both teaching and support staff. We also recommend that the DfE conducts an audit of mental health provision and support within schools, looking at how well the guidance issued to schools has been implemented, what further support may be needed, and highlighting examples of best practice. OFSTED should also make routine assessments of mental health provision in schools. It is clear that education about mental health could and should contribute to prevention and support for young people. We recommend that the DfE consult with young people, including those with experience of mental health issues, to ensure mental health within the curriculum is developed in a way that best meets their needs. (HC 342, 2014, pp. 6–7)

In reality a "should" does not translate to a "must" and government strategies expressed in documents such as *No Health Without Mental Health* (DoH, 2011) and *Closing the Gap: Priorities for Essential Change in Mental Health* (DoH, 2014) have failed to live up to their promise.

A report by National Foundation for Educational Research (NfER, 2016) found that only one third of teachers felt their mental health training was adequate. OFSTED still have no specific requirements for inspectors to report on mental health provision and awareness in schools in spite of additional mental health criteria being added to the OFTSED framework in September 2015.

The value of the "early intervention" allocation received by local authorities fell from £3.2 billion per year in 2010/2011 to £1.4 billion in 2015/2016, a reduction of fifty-five per cent according to the Institute for Public Policy Research (IPPR, 2016). More specifically there has been £85m cuts to Child and Adolescent Mental Health Services (CAMHS) since 2010, £35m of which took place in the last year (Young Minds, 2016). Whatever the churn of government policy in relation to mental health and emotional wellbeing in schools, since the dawn of the new millennium there has been an increasing place for school counselling services, albeit largely provided by the voluntary and charity sector.

Counselling began in schools in the 1960s and has waxed and waned since that time. Currently all secondary schools in Wales, Northern Ireland, and Scotland have a dedicated counselling service and all boarding schools in England are required to have counselling provision. Moreover, in spite of the Department of Health's underlining of the promotion of early intervention in; *Future in Mind: Promoting, Protecting and Improving our Children and Young People's Mental Health and Wellbeing* (DoH, 2015) primary schools across the UK are not statutorily required to have counselling services.

On the brighter side, the Department for Education's (DfE) guidelines: *Mental Health & Behaviour in Schools* (first published June 2014, updated March 2015) positioned schools as pivotal in delivering primary mental health care for children and young people. The DfE's use of the term "Mental Health" might have run the risk of stigmatising some young people who come into the orbit of formal therapies in the setting of school, but overall the document was helpful in contributing to the debate about how a mental health agenda could be embraced and could percolate across professional disciplines, informing teachers and mental health practitioners alike. As far as schools are concerned, we might say that mental health is now everyone's business if not in everyone's budget.

In spite of this somewhat inconsistent picture we know that counselling is valued. For example, ninety-nine per cent of those children in receipt of counselling services in schools in Wales felt they had been understood or helped with their problems and a further ninety-four per cent said that they would definitely go to a counsellor again (Phillips & Smith, 2011). Children value counselling. When counselling services are situated in schools the experience of going to see a counsellor becomes normative; you go to class, you go out to play, you go to the counsellor, you eat lunch. A counsellor can become an ordinary part of school life. A child pays attention to their emotional needs just as they pay attention to their need to eat, play, and learn. It makes sense. Also we know that school attendance and attainment improves post counselling (Daniunaite, Cooper, & Forster, 2015) so it makes sense to governors, head teachers, and teachers alike. The cost to society of a child diagnosed with a conduct disorder is £52,000 by the age of twenty-five according to Barclays Wealth-New Philanthropy Capital (Place 2 Be, 2010), so it makes financial sense when we note that just over half of children with a conduct disorder had improved after a school counselling intervention (Place 2 Be, 2010).

Ten thousand hours of primary mental health care

Schools are where most children from five onwards spend a large part of their waking week. It is where they drag their dreams along with their book bags, where they bring both their fragilities and strengths. For the duration of their time at primary school they spend on average just under 8,000 hours directly with teachers. If you were to include nursery and wrap-around care this would take the figure upwards of 10,000 hours. If you want to identify, understand, and support vulnerable children, then school is about as reliable an access point as you're going to get. School staff are in a unique position to bear witness to and influence a child's emotional wellbeing. Sometimes a class teacher will see more of the child than a working parent, sometimes they will know them better than an estranged father, or a depressed mother, sometimes their understanding, patience, and compassion can be a lifeline. Teaching staff are hugely significant and can act as the custodians of children's welfare and mental health.

Psychotherapists working in schools are also afforded privileged access. They are much less likely to write a "did-not-attend" on their paperwork than their colleagues sitting in a clinic or agency waiting for their client to make the journey across town to meet them. School has good capture, so to speak. OFSTED pays attention to attendance and so it is a priority for schools. If a child doesn't turn up, due to something other than ill health, there is a system that mobilises around them and tries to get them in. All this offers up a great deal of scope and time to identify vulnerable children and impact positively on their lives.

The necessity of early intervention is pressing when we consider that, even by conservative estimations, three children in every classroom will have a diagnosable mental health concern, and one child in every class will have been subject to some form of sexual abuse (Radford et al., 2011). Hospitalisations from self-harm and eating disorders have doubled in the past three years, and in some parts of the country rates of childhood depression, anxiety, self-harm, and eating disorders are up by 600 per cent. The average onset age for depression was forty-five in the 1960s. Today it is fourteen. Either we are getting better at recognising mental distress, or we are failing to create the circumstances to prevent it.

At its best the school system is emotionally resourced by teachers who create a facilitating environment from the classroom to the playground where the therapeutic potential of the school amounts to more than thirty hours a week of contact time. Teachers are crucially positioned to support emotional wellbeing in children. Music (2007) draws attention to a case where several children were referred for counselling from one class, while another class, ostensibly with a parallel population of pupils, had no referrals. Although Music concluded that the discrepancy was due to a differential in teacher experience and capacity to contain disruption in the classroom, there might be more complex dynamics at play when considering the ebb and flow of traffic between different classes and the therapy room. Some teachers are more attuned to the emotional lives of the children and this can afford a greater emotional literacy within the children themselves. It is helpful to look at the story behind the disruptive child.

Nesru, age five, had been admonished for not doing what his teacher asked of him and he was told by the Teaching Assistant (TA) that he needed to say sorry to her. He refused to do this. The TA remonstrated with Nesru but he dug his heels in. The TA offered Nesru the opportunity of writing the word "sorry" instead of having to say it but still he was reluctant to do so. In exasperation she asked, what was the matter? He then gave her an account of what happened leading up to the incident with his teacher. He had been waiting, as instructed, for the staff member who was to support him through his remaining lunchtime. She hadn't turned up and he had waited for her. His teacher then came along and asked him to fall in line and when he didn't the impasse occurred. The TA asked him what he needed to happen to make the current situation better. He said he wanted the staff member who had forgotten to collect him at lunchtime to say sorry. The TA found her and she happily apologised. With this the moral world was asserted, everything fell into place, Nesru was able to accept his part and say sorry, and all concerned were able to get on with their day.

Even very young children are often able to trace the source of their upset if given an opportunity to do so. In the busy life of a school these opportunities are often simply not there but when they are, and there is a sensitive staff member at hand, then the collision between teacher and child can be better understood and solutions can be found. When the child is offered a space to think about his behaviour as part of a network of interactions and antecedents, this process can be installed for future reference. Social justice is a marked feature of young children's lives. Often when there is a reluctance to apologise you will find that the apology is not the child's alone and they, quite rightly, do not want the whole weight of the "wrongness" falling to them alone.

The school psychotherapist needs to maintain a socially contextualised focus of their work, a sort of citizen-ecological view of clinical presentation that is both child focused but collaboratively constructed with regard to working openly with an array of stakeholders. In this system approach, confidentiality is not compromised, but rather fitted to the policy agenda for joined-up approaches to care (DoH, 2004). At best the school psychotherapist is no longer viewed as isolated, distant, and aloof, but rather an integral component of the team and the life of the school. Here it is possible to extend the service beyond one-to-one counselling of children and offer up parent work, teacher support, classroom and playground observations, and a self-referral drop-in service for all the children in the school where any child in the school can come along and have a brief chat about what is troubling them, alone or with a friend. This model facilitates a therapeutic milieu as opposed to a series of singular therapeutic interventions and whilst the remote counsellor might be better able to maintain objectivity, the on-site counsellor is privy to the rich and intersecting emotional lives of the whole school.

Bowlby (1951) pointed out that; "Just as children are absolutely dependent on their parents for sustenance, so ... are parents dependent on a greater society for economic provision. If a community values its children it must cherish their parents" (Bowlby, 1951, p. 84). So we need to consider interconnecting systems to build the good society, and these might be economic bonds as well as emotional. Some teaching staff are brought up and live in the community the school serves. Some have taught the parents and are now teaching their children. Others arrive with an outsider perspective, which can be valuable and challenging. Of course there are teachers who want their job to be just academic performance, they do not want to know about the underbelly of the lives of the children they teach, after all they didn't come into the profession to be social workers or therapists. But there are many teachers who wish they had more time to pay attention to the wellbeing of children. School is where children can bring their whole self. It is the first major community outside of the family for the child. Perhaps where all teachers will agree is that school is a mission in preparation in citizenship.

Talking with a deeply troubled six-year-old client about the impact of her behaviour on those around her, the therapist asked what she thought about her teachers, who incidentally were job sharing. "How do they feel?" replied the client, which made the therapist think that the question had not entirely registered as intended; "one teacher feels love and the other feels sad". Young children can be closer to the truth as they haven't quite mastered the social practices of concealment and defence. She was right, the sad teacher was, indeed, awash with loss and the other teacher was better connected to sources of love at the time.

Children are very intuitive and arguably they are not consulted enough about their lives and the management of their distress. The inclusive format Common Assessment Framework (CAF) often does not invite the young child to attend almost as if being privy to the lives they lead is too much for them. And whilst we must not burden children with decisions which have consequences for which they might feel guilty, we should engage with them as to their perspective on the life they live.

Harry, age five, was sitting at his teacher's feet deciding whether or not to comply with what she was asking of him which was to stay in the classroom and think about how he might have managed the morning differently. All his classmates were outside at play except for Ailsa, who had a cast on her leg and was unable to go out. The teacher restated what was required of Harry and it was clear from observing that he was struggling with deciding which way to go. Harry had a history of running out of or "trashing" the classroom when faced with such choices. As he silently remonstrated with himself his bottom lifted from his heels as if he were about to make the "wrong choice". His classmate, who was sitting near a big box of Lego, had been looking on and interjected that Harry could help her build a special world. The teacher took this offer up and incorporated it into the request, "If you do the right thing you can then play with Ailsa". Harry did precisely that.

Children can intuitively understand when a peer is at a different stage to them, even if they are the same age and in the same class. Three children in Foundation, on a psychological level, in many ways had barely been born and were in early infancy. Their classmates, particularly the girls, would mother them, remind them of class rules, praise them when they had done well. These same children did not extend these behaviours to other, more able children. Often children will tell on one another if they see one of their peers not conforming to the norms of classroom life. Much of the time this is not about getting their peer into trouble, it is more a way of confirming for themselves that these are indeed the rules that govern their existence whilst in class. They act as guardians of classroom culture. In the example above Aisla sees that Harry is at a particular juncture in his decision-making and she throws him a lifeline. She knows that Harry likes building. She knows that often Harry struggles to do what the teachers ask of him. She knows that he can become very distressed when he chooses to run and, in turn, he is handled by staff. She knows these things because she has been a witness to all of this, having known Harry since Nursery. So she helps him climb down from the confrontation. She acts as a good classroom citizen.

Just as one teacher might step into the breach when a colleague is having a difficult moment so too will children support one another. Parents are sometimes heard to complain about troubled children disrupting their child, interfering with their learning. Whilst this should be monitored it must also be noticed that school is a place for socialisation alongside education and that children learn valuable coping strategies for life in the classroom. What better time to foster community cohesion and working together than the early years of school. Each child is a building block to a classroom and school community. Furthermore, if this notion of citizenship is fostered in the primary school it stands a better chance of being translated into the much rockier terrain of secondary school and society beyond.

It is progressive to envisage a social system which recognises the importance of early intervention where mental health issues are seen to be part and parcel of the community of all primary and secondary school life, the school as life in a small dose. That is to say, young people learn that if they are feeling more than ordinarily sad, angry or anxious, you can see a therapist who will help you. But we might consider an even more encompassing agenda where the whole school approach, with an emphasis on healthy peer relationships, social inclusion including enfranchisement, is seen part of an aspirational therapeutic community that holds children and young people across their whole school life.

School as TC—school as community hub

Schools offer an invaluable resource for struggling families. For some children school is the only place they feel truly safe. According to the Office for National Statistics (ONS) as soon as children come into the orbit of a school in the UK they are less likely to die at the hands of another. There have been high profile cases such as Ellie Butler and Daniel Pelka who have escaped the school's protection but on the whole, school is a lifesaver. Tragically, some children and young people also take their own lives. Recently released figures from the ONS (2016) tell us that ninety-eight children between the ages of ten and fourteen have taken their own lives in the last decade in the UK. Thirteen late primary school age children and early secondary school children took their lives in 2014 and a further eleven cases were found to be suspected suicide but concluded; "undetermined". Although we need much more research in this area, anecdotally at least, we know that many school age suicides take place in the holidays when the schools are closed and children are at home, possibly isolated from friends and beyond the containing gaze of teachers and other school staff.

For many years now, schools have been expanding their provision in the form of breakfast clubs and after school activities, offering coverage from 8.00 am–6.00 pm. Schools have not yet been asked to do after hours outreach, but that may be on the horizon. For some families who do not have paid work, the school is one of the few public buildings they enter and many parents will look to the school to seek guidance on how to navigate stressful life events. Often parents look particularly to the Head Teacher of the school as the beacon of hope when times are difficult. For many families, schools broker the space between familial collapse (for example, divorce, bereavement, and trauma) to statutory intervention. When things get difficult for families, when a range of multi-agencies become involved, schools are at best helpfully experienced as on-side advocates based on pre-existing relationships, seen by parents to be operating in the best interests of their children.

Gulliver and colleagues (2010) have drawn attention to the reasons why young people, and perhaps their parents, appear to be reluctant to access services citing stigma, embarrassment and poor mental health literacy as the most significant barriers to help-seeking behaviour. They also noted that there was evidence that the young people who had perceived positive past experiences of mental health support were the ones more likely to seek help when troubled later in life. So providing a positive experience of counselling in primary schools might well be a crucial attribute of a system of early intervention that increases the likelihood of young people seeking help later in the future.

The extraneous circumstances of targeted interventions with an "identified child" who is in distress for whatever reason, needs to be considered against the backcloth of the effect of parental involvement, sibling, and peer relations as well as the effect of teacher and significant other involvement, for example grandparents and extended family members. Even where family therapy is not ostensibly the locus of a programme of intervention, the primary school psychotherapist needs to always keep the family in mind. In the school therapy room it is not so much the case that the family is "always under the couch" as Freud would say, but rather it is the case that the family are always in the sand tray.

Formal psychotherapeutic interventions are usually individualistically orientated under the rubric of humanistic, solution focused, and interpersonal approaches (Lines, 2002). Although group approaches, such as belonging groups or peer support counselling groups, are implemented in some areas (Boulton, 2005), these are less commonplace than individual approaches. However, there appears to be an increase in the flexibility of approach among psychotherapy and counselling practitioners responsive to different local needs reflecting a new ethos of practice that begins with a systemic view of the child's presentation, where old orthodoxies of practice welded to one particular school of thought for example, are modified borrowing from an array of best-fit approaches (Bor, Ebner-Landy, Gill, & Brace, 2002). Developing a greater emphasis on group and peer based work in schools would seem to be a key challenge for school psychotherapists, and also for those who train the workforce.

Some school psychotherapists work directly with the family. Schools can be provocative places for parents, activating their own experience of school. Sometimes drop off and pick up times can be fraught. Inter-parental conflict can overspill into both playground and classroom and this needs to be managed by staff and children alike. The psychotherapist can be mindful of these interactions. We might conceive of the school psychotherapist delivering interventions according to three broad systems within the overall school therapeutic community; (i) children and their peers; (ii) families; (iii) teachers and other professional stakeholders. Mapping formal interventions in these terms is an oversimplification, but the model offers a baseline for examining how these system dynamics interact. The school therapist needs to develop a mental working model of a whole school so that the discrete interventions of counselling and psychotherapy can be held in the context of knowledge of roles and specialisms of other stakeholders. The establishment of a classroom milieu that contains and even heals emotional distress among pupils contributes to educational attainment (Durlak, Weissberg, Dymnicki, Taylor, & Schellinger, 2011; Hall, Hall, & Hornby, 2002; Rutter et al., 1979). Rutter and colleagues (1979) extensive study of pupil achievement and wellbeing demonstrated that "whole school processes" were inextricably linked to favourable outcomes.

Mental health matters are subject to contagion effect, so the school psychotherapist should be alert to patterns, for example a spate of self-harm or increased risk taking activity in the school playground. Working with teachers in order to raise consciousness about emotional needs can subtly reorientate teacher perceptions of children who might otherwise have perceived a child to be badly behaved. The school psychotherapist can contribute to an understanding of the nature of a troubled child. Based on longitudinal research, a range of presenting mental health problems, for instance early onset personality disorder and self-harm, have a tendency to dissipate across time given the conducive conditions for social development and adjustment, with schools playing a central role (Johnson et al., 2000), so the school therapist should be alert to the everyday prevailing therapeutic climate of the school where some children will be helped without formal psychotherapy intervention.

Psychotherapists working in schools will know well that sometimes teacher colleagues can have unrealistic expectations of the outcome of specialist counselling interventions with children. It can be the case that the teacher hopes that a referral to the school psychotherapist will bring about a swift solution of a presenting problem. Though this might be the case in some instances, often the aim for the psychotherapist will be to situate the psychotherapy sessions as an adjunct to the overall support that the teacher brings to their work with the child. One example of a favourable outcome to a process of teacher group consultation was in Brent in a project described by the Department for Education and Schools and the Department of Health as; "a model of good practice" (Music, 2007). Staff from the Tavistock Clinic in London acted as external consultants with the aim of increasing teacher understanding about the underlying meaning of pupil disruptive behaviour and improving the capacity of teachers in identifying children at risk and in need of specialised psychotherapy intervention. After three years, ninety-seven per cent of the teachers (n=120) felt more able to persevere with challenging pupils and eighty-three per cent reported feeling less stressed after talking about their work in fortnightly staff groups. It was surmised that the significantly lower rate of absence among the staff team was also a consequence of the alleviation of stress in the staff group.

By working closely through all levels of the school hierarchy, the psychotherapist can support a whole school approach to mental wellbeing (Jackson, 2002). Working directly with teachers, often in informal discussions, the psychotherapist can contribute to building on the ordinary pastoral skills of any good teacher (Hall, Hall, & Hornby, 2002; Salzberger-Wittenberg, Williams, & Osborne, 1993). The same principles can be applied to interactions with parents. In this sense, the psychotherapist is facilitating therapeutic encounters and a culture of enquiry about wellbeing throughout the school; in the staffroom, the corridors, the classroom, and the playground. The following case vignette illustrates some of the system interactions that can contribute to the development of adapted therapeutic community practice in a primary school.

A case narrative: Citizen Kane

Eight-year-old Kane was referred for therapy in spring term. There were concerns about increasing unruly behaviour that could not be easily managed by the teachers. Kane had been a likeable boy, popular with his peers, and there seemed to be a mismatch between the Kane who was amiable and this new Kane who was increasingly unsettled. He began individual sessions, and there was some good progress made in terms of helping Kane talk about what he was finding difficult. But there seemed to be something stuck in terms of the split between "good Kane" and "angry Kane". Sometimes the school psychotherapist had the feeling that Kane only wanted her to see the good Kane. During one week, the therapist saw Kane sitting outside of the Head Teacher's office on several occasions and when Kane came to his next lunchtime drop-in session she asked him how his week had been. Kane responded, "really good". Now the therapist had a choice; should she tell Kane that she had seen him outside of the Head's office or not? In the end she decided to open up the debate responding; "Oh, has it been really good because I've seen you sitting outside the Head Teacher's office this week so I thought something might have been troubling you?" Kane nodded and a dialogue began.

A few months later Kane's individual sessions were progressing well. One week he also turned up at the drop-in service with his friend Amy. In a conversation with the therapist about counselling, Amy appeared to struggle to gather her thoughts. Kane intervened with, "Amy don't look like her dad, they're not the same colour and everyone's saying he's not her dad". Amy was taken back by Kane's openness but she quickly accepted the rules of engagement and began a hesitant account of her upset. A few days later Amy's mother complained to Kane's teacher that Kane had been saying unkind things about Amy's parents. The teacher referred her to the therapist to discuss the matter further. In the meeting with the mother, the therapist said she felt that Kane was trying to be helpful in the drop-in session, and that perhaps he had opened up a space where the whispers of others could be thought about openly. The mother then talked about the complexities of her family life, and she left the meeting reassured that her daughter's situation was being thought about.

Elsewhere, it was apparent that Kane was beginning to talk the language of therapy; he began to grasp an understanding of emotions and feelings. A teacher told the therapist that Kane had been overheard in the playground talking about how good it was to have a person; "to go talk to about things that bother you". Soon Kane could be relied upon to be making suggestions to his peers that they should go to the drop-in sessions, as he had done with Amy. He became something of an ambassador for the counselling service.

When Kane's teacher struggled to contain him in the class she came to talk to the therapist and together they tried to understand how his early life might be impacting on his behaviours. The counselling manager proposed a formulation which was that the occasions when Kane ended up outside the (male) Head's teacher's office might be considered in light of the recent loss of Kane's father from the family home. The teacher later reported that this understanding had been helpful and Kane's exclusions from class were reduced. Later, when Kane's mother came to the therapist as part of the parent partnership work, the therapy manager was able to make links between Kane's behaviour and the pain of having an absent father. Continuing discussions between the therapist and the teacher yielded further insight about the number of children in the class whose fathers were absent. The teacher decided to allocate a special circle time slot to think generally about fathers, including the presence of stepfathers, encouraging all of the children to be sensitive to the different circumstance of their classmates.

The ear to the emotional life of the school therapeutic community

One of the challenges for the school psychotherapist is to hold in mind the proximity of various relationships around the school. In Kane's case the therapist was able to draw from an array of observations, from her interactions with him, his progress in the sessions, how he was in the playground and the corridors and so on. If the therapist had not brought her observation of Kane sitting outside the Head teacher's office, Kane might have been left feeling that the therapist was colluding with his "best-self", and we can see the important role of peer relations and the ripple effect of encounters. Kane's curiosity agitated an important discussion with Amy that brought her mother to have important conversation with the teacher and therapist. Something was held in mind and here we see elements of a therapeutic milieu rippling across a range of intersecting dynamic events. These elements of dialogue, peer relations, and compassion as they evolve alongside the weave of authority and empowerment start to resemble the frame we can consider under the rubric of a therapeutic community, a culture of enquiry where participants can feel enfranchised.

On the one hand it is necessary for the school psychotherapist to be seen as part of the whole school approach, but realistically, there are periods when the role will feel isolated, where the school psychotherapist may feel marginal. Hinshelwood (1994a) talks about the way in which psychotherapists operate as satellites in large organisations like the National Health Service, whereby the distance serves a function in creating the necessary conditions for being on the one hand close enough to know what is going on, but then again distant enough to offer a fresh pair of eyes. This idea of a satellite psychotherapist seems apposite when it comes to thinking about the role of the psychotherapist working in an organisation such as a school, a pupil referral unit, or a care home. The role can be tricky insofar as the therapist might feel torn between being inside and outside the staff team. Colleagues might feel that the therapist is parachuting in and out for an hour a week with a client, and not having to suffer the long haul challenge of a particularly needy child. There may be some elements of envy or resentment from teacher colleagues that the psychotherapist has less prolonged contact, with a small number of children.

For the school psychotherapist and counsellor, it is helpful to step inside the world of the teacher to take time out for whole class observations before starting with a child in one-to-one counselling. Who runs the school and how they run the school matters. Benign, collaborative, consultative leaders create that culture within the school. Autocratic leaders create a different dynamic within their schools. The governors also have a very defining role. Schools that are a matter of half a mile from one another can serve very different catchments with distinct characteristics. School psychotherapists should walk around the streets of the community they serve.

Anxious children are often micro-readers of mood in a teacher and peers. Children who experience domestic violence, for example, often have a 360 degree attunement to their environment borne out of needing to be hyper alert in their homes, waiting for the voice to rise, the door to slam, the plate to smash. They might be better at hearing changes in intonation, for example, or momentary pauses in the teacher's response. Both might unsettle the child and trigger a behavioural issue which then disrupts the class. These sensitive children are the ones who are most likely to intuitively know something is amiss. A particularly sensitive child came straight up to the school therapist one morning and asked; "What's wrong, the teachers are sad?". She was right, though not apparently visibly upset, the staff had been informed that morning of the death of a colleague and were deeply affected. They emanated a sadness that this child could read for she was particularly literate in reading emotions. The counsellor agreed there seemed to be a sadness that was around the school. This child was responding to a school community event that impacted on all the school and was, indeed, shared by the Head Teacher with the whole school later on that day.

Working, living, learning, and thinking together breeds a unique sociability and counsellors have a history of working with a model of confidentiality that can be too isolating. The school-based psychotherapist should look at the school as a group organism and see the young clients referred as part of a group phenomenon, and see themselves as part of that network of communications. The therapist can be attuned to the way in which emotional debris flies around a classroom where children who are experiencing demanding home lives can be vulnerable to projections. There already is an upsurge in the frequency and range of public mental health issues that will continue to confront all of us in the coming years. As financial resources are shorn in dark economic times, we are yet to see the full impact of the diminished coherence of public health prevention programmes.

So what is to be done to combat this decline into hard times? Into the fray we will see the school system as a political nodal point, a battleground of ideologies where education and welfare are locked in together as they were once before in bygone times. As much as the education system has been the bedrock for mass immunisation programmes that has seen the eradication of any number of terrible diseases, we should likewise consider schools as committed to a full immunisation programme aimed at making significant inroads into mental illness. Imagine what it would be like if schools could be as equipped to deliver mental health prevention programmes just as universally as immunisation. Health and education must be an allied comprehensive public service agenda. School leagues tables in the future may be less concerned with success in terms of exam results, and more concerned with gauging outbreaks of illness and evidence of social cohesion. Where the NHS falls short, as it seems inevitably set to do so, the need for health inventiveness in schools will be vital. To some extent this may be a return to an age pre-NHS, even pre-welfare (from the late 1800s onwards) when education served a role in driving forward a national education agenda that was explicitly the cornerstone of ensuring a basic level of wellbeing for all children. Indeed, perhaps the rise of the NHS took away some of the responsibility of the education system as a focal point for ensuring children's welfare and wellbeing.

Education and health in a time of austerity will require our national education system to re-invent itself out of necessity. A rejuvenation of the idea of what was once called the progressive schools movement, with schools operating as therapeutic communities would seem to be indicated. It is timely then to revisit the idea of a whole school approach and to develop the intrinsic role that the school psychotherapist can play in facilitating a therapeutic milieu where vulnerable young people can be engaged and held. We now exist in post *Every Child Matters* (DfE, 2003) times and the dissolution of the ethos of this agenda is unfolding. Teachers and pupils are already familiar with working alongside educational psychologists, family support workers, CAMHS staff, educational welfare officers, school counsellors, and so on. Now there needs to be a formal recognition of this. Time needs to be allocated to meet the demands of this aspect of teaching, so that mental health is not just the domain of the Special Educational Needs Co-ordinator alone.

The idea of school as therapeutic community needs to be refracted through the challenge of assembling coherency from the remaining partitioned ideologies of education and health. As previously stated, not all teachers are committed to thinking about issues relating to mental distress (Weare, 2004; Winship, 2008). Indeed, Ecclestone and Hayes (2010) have described the emergence of the mental health agenda in schools as a *Dangerous Rise in Therapeutic Education*, though this position seems increasingly marginal. It is timely to consider developing and cohering a whole system approach whereby we can develop schools that can operate as adapted therapeutic communities ensuring the most conducive conditions which will benefit all the stakeholders.

CHAPTER TWO

On noticing—observation as practice

Brief

The capacity to notice what is happening in and around the client is among the first set of skills that a trainee school based psychotherapy practitioner develops in the initial stages of training, and these skills are developed and honed throughout a career. The therapist needs to be imaginatively capacious, that is, develop an ability to hold many different observed elements in mind. The capacity for observation involves seeing events, for instance play activities, or hearing things, such as being able to listen carefully to noise or the intonation of the spoken word as it resonates with emotion is an essential part of empathy and understanding. Finally, the practitioner needs to be able to engage through their sense of smell, or notice changes in temperature or atmosphere as these physical elements combine with the other events of an observation. Taken together, we describe all of these aspects of observation under the rubric of "noticing". This chapter looks at how the skills of noticing are developed and refined during the training of new practitioners, especially through the process of infant and child observations. Furthermore, observation being an essential ingredient of training, the field of infant and child observation has slowly extended its role in terms of research, not only as a useful tool for corroborating known developmental theories such as attachment patterns, but also as a means to generating new hypotheses about child development (Miller, Rustin, Rustin, & Shuttleworth, 1989; Rustin, 1994). Although the anchor for the enquiry is the established technique of mother–infant psychoanalytic observation pioneered by Esther Bick (1964), it is argued in this chapter that the original observation methodology needs to be adapted and extended to be better fitted to the plural and complex demands that face counsellors and psychotherapists working in schools.

Observation as research

As a method for researching child development, infant observation tends towards a highly intimate field of family based study, commonly focusing on mother–infant interactions, usually over a longitudinal time frame. Arguably, infant and child observation has become one of the most honed methods of fine grain qualitative research with a growing number of practitioners versed in the method (Rustin, 1989). Whereas quantitative research is interested in extensive data sets, observation practice has emerged from the long history in psychotherapy research where intensive data is generated from a single case study approach. Freud set the tone for major single case studies, for example "Anna O" in *Studies on Hysteria* (Breuer & Freud, 1895) and then later in his case studies such as the "Rat Man", the "Wolf Man" and "Little Hans". Those single case studies, with their memorable detailed narratives, were the basis of theoretical speculation which colleagues afterwards used as templates for making sense of their own clients with similar presentations. The honed psychoanalytic approach to intense qualitative single case study data became the template for counselling psychotherapy research (Winship, 2007), but also the foundation for other qualitative research approach across the social sciences. Of course single case qualitative methods are subject to criticism for the lack of generalizability, but it might be argued that the production of exacting in-depth psychological data sets provide a precision base for testing and developing hypotheses about mental process, interpersonal psychology and social relations. These hypotheses can then be subject to generalisability when more extensive methods of research are employed. Single observations, when collected together by practitioners and perhaps later published in professional journals, begin to inform a critical mass of intelligence where new theories come into focus.

The origins of psychoanalytic infant and child observation might be traced to Freud's observation of his eighteen-month-old grandson's "cotton reel game". In the game Freud noticed that his grandson dropped the cotton reel over the edge of his cot making the sound of the word resembling "gone" [fort in German], and then the word, "here" when pulling the cotton reel back into sight. When Freud observed his grandson using the same rudimentary descriptors on occasions when his mother left the room and then when she returned, Freud surmised that the game of hide-and-seek with the cotton reel might be an activity whereby the experience of mother leaving and returning was symbolically replayed in the play. That is to say the object play was derived from the subjective experience of the departure and return of mother, and so Freud began to develop a line of thought pertaining to the emotional processes and demands of managing loss.

But it was the pioneering work of Melanie Klein which formed the bedrock of infant observation as a defined and specialist field. In 1955 Klein recalled an early observation of a six-year-old child who was unable to use words to express herself;

> I went into my own children's nursery, collected a few toys, cars, little figures, a few bricks and a train, put them into a box and returned the patient. The child, who had not taken to drawing or other activities was interested in the small toys and at once began to play. From this play I gathered that two of the toys figures represented herself and a little boy, a school mate about whom I had heard before. It appeared that there was something about the behaviour of these two figures and that other toy people were resented as interfering or watching and were put aside. The activities of the two toys led to catastrophies, such as their falling down or colliding with cars. This was repeated with signs of mounting anxiety. At this point I interpreted, with reference to the details of her play. (Klein, 1955. p. 125)

Perhaps the most compelling example of Klein's eye for observation is her analysis of Richard, a ten-year-old-boy who was suffering from a range of anxieties which had been exacerbated by the outbreak of the

Second World War (Klein, 1961). Klein saw Richard for ninety-three sessions over a period of four months, and the work was later published as a book; *Narrative of a Child Analysis*, drawn from her copious and detailed notes which she took after each session. In the narrative account of the work we can see Klein closely observing the detail of her client's play, his behaviours, his drawings, and his words. She combines these behavioural observations with a description of her own responses. The account is compelling, not just as a window to the detail of Klein's technique, but also when we consider the account as a memoir of the horror and exhilaration of war through the eyes of a ten-year-old-boy. Through the observations of Richard's play, Klein is able to illuminate a repertoire of emotional states which are causing Richard distress, and we see how the impact of the events of the war intersect with Richard's anxiety in relation to his immediate family.

We know that Klein's colleagues and students were swayed by her approach which began to open up new understandings of the emotional and mental life of children, and in 1949 Esther Bick, a student of Klein, was appointed head of Child Psychotherapy Training at the Tavistock Clinic. Bick introduced infant observation as a core feature of practitioner training requiring new students to undertake observation of ordinary families with small children, a method that became known as the Tavistock model (Wadell, 2013). The aim of the observation process was to introduce practitioners to the challenge of encountering parent-infant interactions, recalling the events in a seminar afterwards and then applying theory in order to make sense of the observation.

It was during the same period that John Bowlby, a former student of Klein in the 1940s, carried out his groundbreaking World Health Organisation (WHO) study of *Maternal Care and Mental Health* (Bowlby, 1951). Among a range of methods, Bowlby conducted a meta-analysis of global research pertaining to the lives and development of children who had been taken into care. Bowlby described his list of sources as; "classes of evidence" (Ibid, p. 15) and notably he placed "direct observation" ahead of "retrospective case study" (meta-analysis) and "follow-up study". Were Bowlby to repeat his research today he would find it hard to justify "direct observation" at the top of a ranking of choice of methods. Today, direct observation finds itself relegated on the ranking scale behind outcomes follow-up study and meta-analysis (the summary of other case studies). Nonetheless, by privileging of "direct observation" at the top of his tree, Bowlby's WHO report became a persuasive argument which raised consciousness about maternal deprivation. The report lead to a raft of policy and practice changes which influenced the care of children who were either hospitalised, in care homes or nursery care, or in substitute families and so on. We might ponder the paradigm changes in what is assumed to be best evidence.

It was in the afterglow of the WHO work that Bowlby began his collaboration with Mary Ainsworth. Together, they developed the idea for the stranger situation observation procedure (Ainsworth & Bell, 1970) which offered an empirical theory base for the development of what became known as "attachment theory" (Bowlby, 1988). There were other notable contributions to child development theory, for instance Daniel Stern's (1985, 1995, 2000) work where, among other studies, he used a "set situation" research observation method in order to examine mother–child interactions. Colwyn Trevarthen's (1979) work also merits attention insofar as he developed a range of laboratory based audiovisual technologies to observe the subtle emotional exchanges between mother and infant. Trevarthen's techno-observation research revealed profound levels of intuition between the nursing couple and affirmed that there was an array of comprehensible communications between mother and infant, confirming much of what Klein and colleagues had proposed regarding the intersubjective exchange between mother and infant.

Piontelli's (1992) observations of intrauterine life using ultrasound proved groundbreaking in the field of observation studies and demonstrated a remarkable continuity of behaviour before and after birth. Using a longitudinal methodology she followed several cases from foetus to child demonstrating that in each case in-utero sensory experiences, and the rhythms of life before birth, could be seen to traceably shape the personalities of the infants post-partum. Of particular note were Piontelli's in-utero study of twins where twins were observed stroking, bumping, and kissing each other. Piontelli highlighted how the developing world of the foetus was varied and impactful, and she drew attention to how prone the foetus is to external stimuli. In utero, baby sleeps, wakes, tastes changes in the amniotic fluid, shows traits of agitation, baby plays with the umbilical cord, hears sounds, and so on. Piontelli's work offered a sort of sociology of in-utero life and she demonstrated that the boundary between the internal and external world of the newborn child was more fluid than we had previously conceived. Indeed, arguably after Piontelli it is reductionist to talk about nature and nurture as distinct items. We are better to conceive of the self in a ceaseless exchange with "the other" from the beginning, pre-birth. As Winnicott (1960) quipped: "there is no such thing as a baby" (Ibid: p. 587), there is always a mother–child couple, plus the impingements of the outside world.

Impetus for observation training

The governing bodies overseeing the training of child psychotherapists and children's counsellors, for instance; the United Kingdom Council for Psychotherapy (UKCP), the Association of Child Psychotherapists (ACP), the British Association of Counselling and Psychotherapy (BACP), and the British Confederation of Psychotherapists (BCP)—all have infant and child observation as a curriculum requirement for practitioner preparation. Psychotherapy registering bodies vary in how much time they allocate for infant and child observations, but the minimum would usually be one observation per week, over a period of twelve months. There are also other trainees in nearby professional fields that undertake an infant-child observation component in their training, for instance midwives, nursery nurses, social workers (Briggs, 2002; Miller, Rustin, Rustin, & Shuttleworth, 1989). The aim of infant and child observation is to develop practitioner skills in noticing aspects of childhood development and early interaction patterns between children and parents, siblings, peers, and significant others.

The setting may be an observation of an infant, child or young person, either in their own home, or in a nursery, school or other setting where there can be regular contact. The observation may also take the form of an internship in a clinic, or shadowing another practitioner in the course of their everyday work. Traditionally infant child observation focuses on a single observee, but there have been some innovations in developing a more group based focus, shifting attention to dimensions of social or group psychology (Winship, 2001). The research paradigm most closely fitted to the procedure of the observation process would be described as naturalistic with an added dimension of the observer attempting to absorb the accompanying emotional content of what is being observed. When conducting an observation, for instance in the setting of a nursery, trainees are encouraged not to take notes during the observation time, instead to record afterwards in a written account, detail of the events of the observation. These findings are then presented at a weekly infant observation seminar where peers listen to each other's observations and are then encouraged to map the findings onto theories of child development.

The observation learning process aims to increase the student's ability to notice the emotional nuance of interactions, to see if across time there are patterns, and then to practice and develop the tools of data recall and note keeping after the event. The settings for observation may vary from studying early mother–infant interaction from birth, through to the child in the setting of the family, and then in the environment of the nursery or school. The duration of the weekly observation is usually an hour or so. Infant observation trainings commonly run over a period of two years, with some expert practitioners, such as parent-infant psychotherapists, undertaking observations in a range of settings including special settings like intensive care neo-natal units. The observation learning cycle is commonly a longitudinal process that includes weekly observations followed by theoretical review. The observation seminar group offers a stimulating forum where students have an opportunity to present their observations and a chance to test out ideas clarifying known theories. Where indicated, in the absence of adequate prior theory, the seminar might generate some fresh hypotheses about child development and the emotional life of infants, children, and young people. The seminar group offers an opportunity for students to calibrate their subjective responses to their observations, especially where seminar members arrive at different opinions and responses to the observable events. An experienced seminar leader might well look for clues as to how far the seminar group dynamics might be mirroring, through a process of re-enactment, the unspoken dynamics of the observation field. The inter-relations in the seminar group might well become one of the key resources of the observation learning cycle.

The responses of observers in the seminar group can be considered in terms of projective identification or countertransference. That is to say, the observer might find themselves identifying with various players in the observation field (the mother, the child, the siblings, the father, the teacher, and so on), experiencing some heightened emotional responses as a result. On occasions the observer might bring some strong emotions into the seminar group, for example feeling distressed because they feel as though they should have intervened during the observation to sooth a distressed child, or to counsel a beleaguered parent or teacher. The role of detached observer can be difficult to maintain, but far from these challenging emotional responses to the observation being seen as impinging, we might see them as a valuable resource for the learning cycle.

Taken together, infant and child observations offer a fruitful grounding which prepares the new practitioner for their practice as novice psychotherapist insofar as the observer is faced with the hour long observation without taking notes, and then the challenge of recalling and recording the events of the observation in detail. The observer, like the practicing psychotherapist, needs to monitor their personal emotional response to the encounter reflecting on the meld of subjectivity and objectivity.

The child's social matrix

Counsellors and psychotherapists working with children and young people are invariably situated proximal to a wide array of other stakeholders in the lives of their young clients. A child exists in the constant flow of an array of relationships from parents to siblings, to extended family, to school peers and teacher and then the wider community. The range of external agents will sometimes span outwards from teachers to include social workers, doctors, police, and so forth. We might call this "the child's social matrix". The school psychotherapist needs to develop a capacity to notice and understand the network around the client. This is the essence of a joined up approach where the child is seen not in isolation, but as a part of wider family and social system.

So how might we develop the observation method that extends the Bick method of dyadic observation to embrace an approach that pays more heed to the social matrix? Of note is the work of Susan Isaacs. Isaacs has a quiet but well considered place in psychoanalytic history (several books, thirty scientific papers) but in the chronicles of nursery education in the UK she is considered something of a radical pioneer (Gardener, 1969; Woodhead, 1976). In 1924 she established the Malting House school, where she organised an experimental structure in order to facilitate the children's education through a liberal and essentially emancipating approach to learning. It was out of this experience that she published her first major book; *The Nursery Years* (Isaacs, 1929). Her work at Malting House became so influential that Jean Piaget, reported he was led to use fresh techniques in his own investigations after he visited Isaacs' school (Gardener, 1968, p. 68). Isaacs asserted that it was the social aspects of a situation that were crucial in influencing the behaviour of an individual child. For instance, who was present when a certain emotion was displayed and what was happening with the other children at the time (Isaacs, 1933; 1952). Her effort to conjoin social study with psychoanalysis in the context of nursery observation is of particular interest here insofar as she developed a technique of coding data and drawing of inferences in a way that would seem to be a prototype for a method of contextual observation (Isaacs, 1933).

Somewhat independently of Isaacs, the work of Anna Freud is likewise notable because through her work in establishing toddler groups, "well-baby clinics", and nursery care programmes during the 1940s working with "transporter children" as they were known, children who had displaced from their families as a result of the Second World War. Anna Freud's interest in peer relationships was fuelled because many of the children she worked with were orphaned and the absence of parents had led the children to become precociously peer orientated. Anna Freud attended to both the emergent sociality and emotionality of the young children. For instance in observing the play of a group of young children she noted;

> Sam (20 months) was playing peacefully … when suddenly Larry (19 months) took his ball away. Sam looked at his empty hands help-lessly and began to cry. Edith (21 months) had watched this scene; she rushed over to Larry, bit him, brought the ball back to Sam, and stroked his hair until he was comforted. (Freud & Burlingham, 1944, p. 573)

In contrast to Klein, who was concerned primarily with the child's relationship with mother, Anna Freud was interested in peer relations, a more horizontal focus we might say.

In the task of observing a group situation, for example in a playground where there are numerous children, the observer is presented with an immediate challenge of visual engagement. Whereas observing one child the optical field of study is restricted and manageable, when the observation multi-bodied with older children who are mobile, the space of observation becomes more fluid, less centred. The perceptual limit of the observer's faculties means that it is impossible to attend to all events. The observer might aim to find a position where as much of the observation field can be seen. Initially directing their gaze towards the centre of a room or space, the observer follows events as they occur outwards from there. For example if one child in an observation is upset the observer should attempt to monitor the impact on others in the observation field rather than focusing only on the focal encounter. In short, the visual field or space of the observation is as important as the dramatis personae.

In considering the concept of the space of the observation some of the following ideas might be reference points, for example Winnicott's (1951) notion of "transitional space" which pertains to the interim space that facilitates the child in his movement away from his mother. The idea of transitional space might have some resemblance in Lacan's (1960) concept of "l'objet a" which is a concept concerned with the absence of an object which leads to a desire to fill the space with something else. Also Balint's (1968) differentiation between "ocnophilic" and "philobatic" contact in object relations which refers to the idea of space in-between objects as much as the objects themselves, and Segal's (1991) concept of "mental space", that is to say the absence of the mother that leads to early symbol formation and creativity. Rey's (1994) thinking about space is also apposite when he discusses the movement from maternal space to "marsupial space" (Rey, 1994, p. 21). By marsupial, Rey is thinking about the maternal pouch in marsupials where the baby makes a soft transition between in-utero existence and the outside world. Rey proposes that ordinary human mothering might be said to resemble this marsupial model of child development where there is an interim phase of movement for the child whereby inside space becomes partially outside space with baby closely swaddled. Finally, Hinshelwood's (1994b) concept of reflective space between minds, which he applies to inter-subjective experiences in group settings, drawing attention to the concept of the psychic space between people.

In undertaking observations of the "social matrix" that surround the child in the setting of a school, the observer will be challenged to absorb a wide range of informational experiences. The precise data that is gathered can be presumed to be only a fragment of the multiplicity of events taking place. The observation might be described as an organic process whereby the sense faculties of the observer are a conduit for the nuanced array of events taking place. That is to say, the observer may observe the smell of food or faeces, or the sound of an aeroplane passing overhead, the telephone ringing or a car pulling up on the drive or how a draft created by the opening of a door, or the breeze from a window changes the temperature and the inter-textual experience of those in the observation space. The observation approach might be fundamentally receptive to bio-emotional states (Liekerman, 1995), a type of sensory-organic engagement in the process of structuring of experience whereby the interaction between the observer's mental internality and sensual externality is combined in the process of reflection. It is an approach that does not actively seek to gather data, but rather is more a state of being with the observation that attempts not to impede the ingestion of experience; observational alchemy we might call it. The observer, in a sense, aims to watch less in an attempt to notice more. We could consider this effort of noticing as a process of accessing the optical unconscious (Krauss, 1994). For example, if we look at 3D pictures (Magic-Eye art books for instance) at first one can only see a surface pattern of colours, no shape is apparent and the picture appears to be a single dimension. With practice and perseverance one can develop an ability to relax and look almost beyond the surface of the picture, where a 3D image appears. The image emerges upwards, apparently from nothing. This experience is quite uncanny, particularly because one does not always know what image will emerge. It is also the case that the harder one tries to see beyond the surface of the 2D pattern, the less likely you are to see the 3D image. This is how it is with the unconscious—it is more common that in our most relaxed state of sleep that we are able to see the unconscious depicted. In recording the data the observer seeks to remain as faithful as possible to the chronology of occurrences, resisting the inclination to encode the data prematurely to fit into preconceived theoretical axioms. Rather, the observer writes the narrative of the observation, detailing facts and subjective responses, which are taken into supervision where the process of mulling over the data with peers and supervisor attempts to find theoretical fit.

Observations in a primary school

The following section provides an example of an observation undertaken by a school psychotherapist who, by matter of routine, undertook classroom and playground observations ahead of a new client commencing therapy. In the observation account we see how the psychotherapist not only collected her thoughts about what was happening, but also how she intervened. The observation procedure in this case became part of the process of intervention.

The therapist went to observe five-year-old Malika in the school nursery. Malika was a third generation child or African heritage. Malika had just returned from being excluded after repeatedly biting and hurting other children, and disruptive behaviours such as overturning tables and chairs. The therapist arrived to find Malika moving bits of paper around a table. All the other children had just seated themselves for music and the teacher was reminding Malika that she had been asked to tidy away and move over to the shared area ready for the music. Instead, Malika moved over to the sinks nearby and started washing her hands vigorously under a rushing tap. She continued doing so in spite of the teacher's remonstration for her to bring her hand washing to an end and join her friends.

After Malika had finished washing her hands, she began cleaning the sink itself. She then noticed that water from her sink had splashed into the next sink, so she then started to clean that sink with equal vigour. Next she started cleaning the third sink with a blue paper towel. The teacher had been reiterating what she needed Malika to do at various intervals to no avail so she finally took the paper towel from Malika and put it in the bin. Malika then started running around the room. She went to some curtains and wrapped herself in them until she couldn't be seen. The teacher came and unwrapped the curtains reminding Malika that it wasn't safe. Malika then climbed on to the low windowsill and looked out for a moment. The teacher picked her up and put her on the ground telling her it wasn't safe. Once Malika had circled twice she slowed down somewhat and crawled on the ground sniffing as she went. She then got up and started looking underneath various objects, a basket, a pile of papers, under a shelf.

The teacher knelt down and asked Malika to come to her, which after a moment or so, she did. Malika started talking about her birthday and the teacher told her that it wasn't her birthday, but when it was she was going to bring her; "a special balloon". At this point the observing therapist interjected and said to Malika; "And who else was there on your birthday, the day you were born?" The therapist then turned to the teacher and said; "I wonder if Malika is missing her mummy?" Malika turned to the therapist and said; "Yes, I miss my mummy, I can smell her but she's not here." Malika then sat down and said; "there is a man in my brain who is angry and tells me what to do. I can't get away from him". She went on to say that she thought this man was going to eat her, the teacher, and the whole classroom. The teacher said; "I wonder what we can do to stop the man in your brain, bothering you". After this, Malika sat down with the rest of her classmates, and drank her beaker of milk. The observation continued for another fifteen minutes, in which Malika remained engaged with her classmates, and was reportedly fine for the remainder of the morning.

In reflecting on the observation, and pooling further information gleaned from an initial interview with Malika's mother ahead of therapy commencing, it was possible to begin a working formulation or hypotheses about Malika's activities during the observation. Malika was asked to tidy away. Tidying away suggested that something was coming to an end. Now maybe Malika simply didn't want to tidy up, after all, many children are reluctant to do so, but children are generally compliant so when a very young child is prepared to stand out from her peers and defy adults in authority, we might speculate that something of an imperative nature had overridden her need for approval and the desire to belong. When the teacher made the request of Malika to tidy up, Malika might have experienced anxiety and was not able to join with her peers. Might we frame this in terms of separation anxiety and attachment theory? When Malika got down on her hands and knees and began sniffing, is it possible that she was looking for her mother as if she hadn't quite acknowledged her leaving the building? We know that a secure base is necessary for a child to make a transition away from mother, and when the base is not secure there can be problems (Bowlby, 1988). It was certainly true for Malika that her early life was marked by anxiety, uncertainty, and an angry, violent father.

Although the "angry man" was no longer in her life, there was a strong residue of fear accompanied by his recent presence. Perhaps the thought needed to cleansed and washed away. Malika's thoughts might have splashed into the nearby sink. But when she tried to clean away the thoughts of the angry man, she found her thoughts splashing into the next sink leaving Malika with a major clean up job. She was unable to relinquish this cleaning up process until the teacher intervened. She then felt exposed or frightened and tried to wrap herself in the curtains, seeking containment. She then climbed and looked out of the window, perhaps searching for her mummy. Perhaps she needed to know her mummy had survived an attack, albeit imagined in this moment, from the angry man. The holding from the teacher, as she plucked Malika from the window sill was all too fleeting and Malika ran in circles, denoting her failure to get anywhere and make the situation better. Notably, Malika's unsettled activity began to de-escalate following the exchange about birthdays, and the observer's comment about missing mummy. Malika was able to exercise her mind and talk about the thoughts that were bothering her. Her actions were replaced by words and she calmed down.

As a training method, the process of observation is intended to be unobtrusive whereby the student gathers intelligence, but does not respond. In the above observation the therapist intervened, albeit a minimal interjection, but it nonetheless appeared to be helpful and containing. Some days later, the therapist had the opportunity to meet with nursery school staff to gather a fuller picture of Malika. The nursery staff had many demands on their time and Malika was quite a challenge for them. What emerged was a complex picture with Malika being seen as needy, and some staff saw her as "attention seeking", "manipulative", and "defiant". She was also seen as bright, funny, and engaging. One of her most worrying behaviours was her climbing, which resulted in staff having to pick her up and carry her.

Based on her observations and what she had come to know of Malika from individual sessions, the psychotherapist told the nursery staff that she thought that Malika might be frightened and that she engineered situations whereby she would need to be physically held by the staff. Some of the nursery staff were persuaded by the idea and later managed Malika's risky behaviour by acknowledging her vulnerability, while other staff seemed to prefer the advice that they had received from the Early Years Coordinator that, on the occasion of Malika's risky climbing behaviour she would be removed from the shared area to stand alone without eye contact or touch. Sometimes trying to understand these behaviours can be perceived by some school staff as trying to excuse these behaviours, so the split in the staff's response to the therapist's thoughts might sound familiar. Over the subsequent months however, there was some improvement. Some of the staff continued to use isolation in response to Malika's behaviour, but Malika became more grounded and needed less intervention. We might say that a shift in the perception of the staff yielded real change in Malika.

Reflections—developing the social matrix observation method

There are precedents for extending the Tavistock observation method, with its primary focus on mother–infant interactions, to embrace a method of observation that pays heed to diverse settings where more socially focused data can be culled, social matrix observations as we have called it. For example, Mackenzie-Smith (1992) widened her frame in her observations of elderly patients interacting with staff on a geriatric hospital ward, while Chiesa (1993) conducted a study of an acute psychiatric inpatient unit focusing his observation not on any single individual, but rather observing the general events and prevailing atmosphere of a ward. Hinshelwood & Skogstad (2000) likewise reported on a number of observation studies carried out in a range of health settings including hostels, psychiatric units, and general hospital settings where the focus was on a social collective rather than on an individual.

A child's social matrix grows from the building blocks of early family experiences and extends to peer relating capabilities in schools. School is arguably the most important fundamental influence on the child's experience of social matrix beyond home. Although some would argue that group relating capabilities are absent in children until the age of two years, it is possible to hypothesise a developmental line for peer relatedness beginning long before two years of age. Atkins (1983) noted that that the early play of children in group situations had been virtually ignored as the location of emerging social relationships. He undertook to show from a series of observations that inter-relatedness during the first year of life was not just reflexivity or response by contagion, as Piaget (1951) believed, but that peers had an important role to play. Our hunch is that the development of social matrix observations, which draws on the Tavistock method, but looks at the wider dynamic network of the child in the school, provides three essential ingredients for the field of child psychotherapy; (i) as a method for practitioner training which introduce the range of skills that are required as a practitioner; (ii) as a tool which can illuminate therapeutic intervention, as in the case of Malika above where the psychotherapist was able to get a wider picture of the child before commencing individual therapy; and (iii) as a method for empirical social research which extends our knowledge of child development and the challenges of working with troubled children.

CHAPTER THREE

On relating—attachment and belonging

Brief

This chapter looks across the field of attachment theory and practice. Theory is illustrated with an extended case study where matters of a disorganised attachment were replayed in the work with a nine-year-old child. In the case account we can see how attachment theory was a basis to understanding some co-occurring dynamics, in particular the transgenerational transmission of trauma. Further, we consider the nature of attachment to peers both in and outside of school, taking a look at the notion of community, citizenship, and belonging. We argue that understanding attachment theory is an essential ingredient for all counsellors and psychotherapists working in primary schools, and also that it is a helpful idea for parents trying to understand their relationship with their children. Finally, getting to grips with attachment can be useful for teachers in aiding them in relationship building with children across a period of time.

Impetus

John Bowlby (b 1907), the father of attachment theory, has continued to find voice not only in psychotherapy practice but also in health service, education, and childcare provision in the UK and abroad. Attachment theory grows in stature and utility decade upon decade culminating, more recently, in a concerted effort to integrate some of its insights into teaching practice itself. Teach First, the Universities Council for the Education of Teachers (UCET), the National Association of School-Based Teacher Trainers (NASBTT), and the Teaching Schools Alliance, are among the organisations who have been working together to promote attachment based practices, generating guidance and policy steer for teacher education.

In 2014 the Consortium for Emotional Well-Being in Schools (CEWB) launched a new report at the House of Commons which highlighted the inadequacy of current education provision for teachers in terms of developing an understanding of the emotional demands and attachment needs of children and young people. The report was the outcome of round table discussions convened by Francis Earl Listowel in the House of Lords which brought together research academics, senior representatives of national children's organisations, trainers, school leaders, and practitioners. The CEWB report set out guidance for the way in which attachment theory could shape the work of schools with opportunities for all those working in schools to have access to accredited training in children's emotional development with attachment theory as a core idea. Sir Andrew Carter was involved in the CEWB launch and in his 2015 report on Initial Teacher Training (ITT) he stressed the importance of understanding child and adolescent development:

> ITT should provide new teachers with a grounding in child and adolescent development, including emotional and social development, which will underpin their understanding of other issues such as pedagogy, assessment, behaviour, mental health and SEND. ITT should also introduce new teachers to strategies for character education and supporting pupil wellbeing. (Carter, 2015, p. 23)

Attachment Aware Schools, co-ordinated from Bath Spa University, is a growing network of organisations and practitioners who have been applying attachment theory to practice, noting that secure attachment is a cornerstone of improved academic performance, and also is a basis for considering how to help children who are struggling (www.bathspa.ac.uk/education/research/attachment-aware-schools/). Attachment theory (Bowlby, 1969) and the sister concepts of separation

(Bowlby, 1973) and loss (Bowlby, 1980) can help teachers appreciate the differing experience that shape the way children communicate and behave. Attachment, separation, and loss, offers an indispensable framework which can throw light on how children transition from home to school, and also transitional behaviours within school as children move from one space to another, classroom to playground, lesson to lesson. It also provides a frame within which to understand how children relate to their peers and authority figures. However, Bowlby's ideas were not developed without controversy and it is helpful here to offer up a brief biography of attachment theory's early days and the influences that shaped Bowlby's perspective.

John Bowlby undertook a degree in 1925 in preclinical sciences and psychology at Cambridge before studying clinical medicine at University College Hospital, London. He spent 1929 as a teacher in a school for troubled children where he learned about the work of A. S. Neill and the Summerhill School which was applying psychoanalytic and democratic philosophy to working with challenging children and adolescents. It was this experience of progressive schooling that began to shape Bowlby's interest in child development. Bowlby completed his medical training in 1933 and then went on to complete his psychiatric training at the Maudsley Hospital, London, finally qualifying as a psychiatrist in 1937. He immediately embarked on his training as a child analyst, working in the London Child Guidance Clinic and also at the Institute of Psychoanalysis, London.

In 1950, the World Health Organization (WHO) invited Bowlby to advise on the mental health of homeless children. The findings of this WHO study seemed to confirm his earlier findings from working with deprived children. The study took Bowlby to Europe and the United States and was completed in six months. The findings were published under the title of *Maternal Care and Mental Health*, although they later became known as *Child Care and the Growth of Love* (Bowlby, 1953) when additional material was added. The study was a landmark piece of research, where Bowlby focused on gathering emotional data rather than economic, medical, or social, which was commonplace at the time. Bowlby coined the term; "maternal deprivation", explicating the damaging effects caused by the loss of mother (or the absence of adequate mothering) on the child's developing personality. He concluded that warm, intimate, and continuous relations with the mother (or permanent mother substitute) in which both mother and infant found satisfaction and enjoyment, were an essential basis for longer-term mental health. Among other conclusions, Bowlby drew attention to the neglected child, with psychopathic and delinquent tendencies, growing up to become a neglectful psychopathic parent, a self-perpetuating, destructive cycle.

Bowlby saw himself primarily as a researcher, and his academic interests stretched his horizons beyond psychoanalysis as he drew widely from other disciplines, including Darwinian evolution, systems theory, cybernetics, human information processing, and comparative psychology. He took to scientific pluralism with gusto and made a case that the time was ripe for a unification of psychoanalytic concepts with those of the natural sciences. He took a particular interest in relating ethology (the study of animals in their natural environment) to psychoanalysis. Ethology opened up new possibilities for Bowlby in his research into the development of mother–offspring bonds and the impact on the infant of separation. Harlow's (1958) ethological studies of rhesus monkeys struck a resonance with Bowlby's earlier speculations. Harlow had set up an experiment where he had constructed two surrogate mothers. The first "mother" was made out of wire and had a feeding bottle, while the other "mother" was covered in soft cloth minus the feeding bottle. In the experiment, the monkeys attached themselves to the; "soft mother". Likewise, Bowlby noted parallels in the work of Konrad Lorenz on imprinting in goslings. In 1935 Lorenz had found that goslings would follow their mother or mother substitute without the promise of food, becoming distressed when physically separated from her. Based on the study of animals, Bowlby produced a neo-Darwinian schema for understanding the primitive need for the infant to stay close to its mother.

As a result of this work, Bowlby pressed for government funding to be redirected from institutions into the domestic sphere to support parents who were struggling in the absence of necessary support and provision. However, his emphasis on the importance of the mother offering continuous care, which Bowlby called "monotropy", was considered inflammatory by many women. Bowlby was accused of tying woman to the home and motherhood (see Chodorow, 1978, for a fuller discussion), arguably a criticism that remains salient today.

Concurrent with these developments was the work of Mary Ainsworth, a Canadian psychology graduate who was influenced by William Blatz's (1940) "Security Theory" which identified an infant's need to feel secure before moving away from mother to explore the world.

In 1950 Ainsworth applied to work under Bowlby in London as part of a research team investigating infant separation from the mother. During this time Bowlby collaborated with James Robertson, a social worker, who worked at the West Hampstead Nursery run by Anna Freud in London. Robertson had become attuned to the effects on children of institutionalisation and separation from their mothers and in order to bring this to the attention of the general public, Bowlby encouraged Robertson to make a film. The result was, *A Two-Year-Old Goes to Hospital*, which was first screened in 1953 at the Institute of Psychoanalysis, and then shown on the BBC in 1956 (Robertson, 1953). The film was a paradigm changer, bringing child centred psychoanalytic psychology to public consciousness.

Bowlby concluded from his studies with Robertson that distress in a child over six months of age was due to loss of maternal care at a time when the child was highly dependent and at a vulnerable stage of development. He stated that the young child's hunger for his mother's love and presence was as great as his hunger for food, and that her absence generated a powerful sense of loss and anger. Ainsworth refined and then tested these ideas creating a social experiment called; The Strange Situation Test. The study involved the unobtrusive observation of a mother and infant who were situated in a playroom laboratory, joined a short while later by a female stranger. The stranger then played with the baby, while the mother left the room briefly returning a few minutes later. A further separation was introduced whereby both mother and stranger left the infant alone in the room. Finally, the stranger and then the mother return.

Ainsworth found that infants explored the playroom and toys more robustly in the presence of their mothers than after a stranger entered or while the mother was absent (Ainsworth & Bell, 1970). However, other reunion behaviours emerged which echoed the Robertson separation studies which Bowlby (1959) had theorised in his paper on separation. A handful of children were angry when their mother returned and refused comfort, some hitting their mother. Others behaved as if they had not noticed the mother's return although in her absence it was clear that they were looking for her. On further case by case scrutiny it was revealed that there was a correlation between the mother–infant relationship at home and the observations noted in the Strange Situation Test, for example where the mother–infant relationship was more troubled at home, the infants in the test were less able to express their sadness at their mothers absence and less able to receive comfort from her when she returned (Ainsworth, Bell, & Stayton, 1974).

Thus originated the Strange Situation classification system (Ainsworth et al., 1978) whereby a range of attachment patterns were noticed, including: (i) secure, (ii) insecure avoidant, and (iii) insecure ambivalent, each with descriptors that provided a formula for further testing and clinical assessment. Another category called "disorganised attachment" was added to the classification system in 1978. Ainsworth and colleagues argued that there was evidence which pointed to patterns of attachment, for example where a child had experienced erratic care-giving, they would typically form an insecure-ambivalent-avoidant attachment. Ainsworth's student Mary Main especially became interested in parental attachment styles (Main & Solomon, 1986). Main noticed that some mothers appeared to be frightening and subsequently their children presented with a disorganised attachment. With this additional category she started paying closer attention to the mother's story and attachment style and this ultimately resulted in her developing the Adult Attachment Interview (AAI), which provided a protocol for assessing the attachment style of the mother. Broadly speaking, AAI research concluded that the coherence of a parent recounting their own history predicted how they would relate to their child and consequently how the infant would respond in the Strange Situation (Hesse, Cassidy, & Shaver, 2008).

Attachment applied

Attachment theory has received criticism for being too reliant on a westernised notion of parenting and that it does not easily account for cultures where parenting a child takes place within a wider community, for instance in kibbutz or in extended family systems. However, Bowlby and his attachment research colleagues did firmly put in place the importance of the environment and the primary importance of the mother herself, and the necessity of a secure base for healthy child development (Bowlby, 1988). Bowlby concluded that mother love was as important for mental health as vitamins and proteins were for physical health. Attachment theory had significantly advanced the understanding of human personality development and the dangers of cycles of deprivation. In concrete terms, the findings from Bowlby's research began to significantly shape not only policy and practice with sick children, but also hospital design. He catalysed the transition from restricted visiting in hospitals where parents were experienced as something of a nuisance on the paediatric ward, to the development of a principle that parental involvement and proximity were actually crucial in actively improving outcomes for the sick child. Specially built rooms and accommodation to meet the demand for maintaining parental contact wherever possible became the gold standard and continues to this day.

Interest in attachment intensified with numerous elaborations to the core theories. Attachment disorders began to be classified in the *Diagnostic and Statistical Manual* (DSM5) and in the *International Classification of Diseases* (ICD10) which delineated two types of Reactive Attachment Disorder; (i) inhibited: where the child does not seek out social contact when distressed and does not find comfort in caregivers and; (ii) disinhibited where children are profligate in their sociability and they are indiscriminate with whom they share affections. Although Bowlby neglected to study the first six months of the infant's life, there has been, and continues to be, an increasing sensitivity to the very early emotional life of the infant including prenatal (Piontelli 1992; Ploye, 2006). Today we might consider the foundational placenta or umbilical attachment as the template for all that follows, and indeed therapists might well encounter children born to mothers who experienced domestic violence when pregnant, and in turn, the child might manifest difficulties in light of these formative experiences. Further, with the increase in survival rates from premature births, which are more prevalent in those experiencing deprivation, a significant part of gestational life can take place outside of the womb and the implications of this in relation to bonding and attachment need might be considered in terms of what we call an "incubator psyche" (MacDonald, 2015).

So how can attachment theory be useful in practice? The following accounts offer illustrations of how a range of attachment based ideas can frame our understanding of some of the difficulties that young children bring to therapy. When four-year-old Bethany first started attending nursery it was not uncommon for her face to be tear streamed. Saying goodbye to Mummy each morning was a separation ritual that was painful and difficult to bear for Bethany and her mother. But it was usual after some minutes that Bethany would settle, and she would adapt to her environment. The more that the separation, and the reunion became routinised the better able Bethany was able to manage the separation, and after a few weeks, she ceased crying at the point of separation.

Within months she was able to engage fully with the routine of the nursery and she demonstrated resourcefulness and resilience, engaging with her peers. By dint of contrast, when four-year-old Tao arrived at nursery he appeared to show no difficulties in separating from his mother, or sometimes his older sister who dropped him off. He would bluster into play and his mother or sister would disappear without as much as a second look. However, Tao seemed to find it difficult to engage with the other children, his play didn't seem to be mutual and he didn't seem to be invited into peer games. When it came to quiet time, either for drinks, biscuits or a story, Tao did not seem able to slow down and his relationships with others became fractious, both with his peers and with the nursery staff who would get frustrated with Tao's inability or unwillingness to follow their instructions.

Where children have not had the experience of a secure base they often find it really difficult to separate from their parent and get on with the school day. These kinds of scenarios require a different approach from school staff and the move toward independence needs to be put on hold until a period of dependence is facilitated. The school therapist can often be that steady person that the child attaches to whilst working out the challenges and vagaries of the social field. One of the most helpful frames in which to understand the struggling child is to look at the stage they are at rather than the age. Some children begin school at four or five and yet developmentally and emotionally they might be barely more than a baby or toddler. So a child who is behaving in a way where, say, the teacher ends up holding and handling them a lot, whilst all their peers can be managed by voice and instruction alone, this might give an indication that they are not the same developmental age as their peers. This is when therapists and teachers need to work closely together in supporting the child as they are often under threat of exclusion for being unable to meet age appropriate classroom expectations.

Attachment and ASD

Whilst attachment theory governs the behaviours of the child, we find the notion of "attachment between" helpful. Therefore it is often the relationship between the mother and the child that comes into focus when the counsellor is assessing what is so unsettling for a child who is struggling to transition between spaces, both psychological and physical. Attachment theory is as much a spatial theory as it is a relational one as it maps intrapsychic and inter-psychic spaces between. Attachment difficulties have transgenerational tributaries and therefore it is useful to enquire as to the nature of the child's mother's relationship to her mother and school as a child. We might say there is no such thing as a transitioning child only a transitioning couple. If a child picks up that mother is anxious and ambivalent about letting the child go to school then this does not lend itself to a smooth handing over of the child into the care of another. The depressed mother might not be available and able to do the transitioning that is required to temporarily separate from their child. These are sometimes characteristics of the mothers who linger at the classroom and find opportunities to come into school as they feel they have left something of themselves there.

It is not uncommon to happen across children with a diagnosis of Autistic Spectrum Disorder (ASD) who have profound attachment difficulties that feel existential in nature. For attachment to take place there needs to be some acknowledgement that the figure to whom you attach is "over there", so to speak. In other words an infant needs to be able to conceptualise that they are distinct from mother in order to attach to her. Tustin (1982) argued that all children with autism experience a traumatic realisation of separateness which drives them into an autistic retreat. We might refer to this as an adhesive attachment where there is not enough space in between for individuation to take place and a sense of being a separate "I". This absence of an "I am" also inhibits the scope of attachment to peers, there is no "I" as the necessary basis to seek out others. For these children navigating horizontal and vertical relationships which govern school life can be very problematic as they are confused as to their place in the world.

Six-year-old Sony was referred to the therapist because the school teachers were at their wits ends. When Sony had to move from one class to another or from one activity to another, his cries would reverberate through the school each and every day. When the therapist spoke to Sony's mother Janie, Janie told the therapist that they had recently moved house, but that Sony had not seemed to grasp that they had moved. Apparently, on the way to school Sony would try to find the zebra crossing where they used to cross, or he would look for the lamp post on the brow of the hill, both of which were features of their previous locale. The therapist asked Janie what she thought this might mean. Janie said that when Sony was a baby he had never cried. At first the therapist couldn't make a link between the house move and Sony not crying as a baby, it seemed tangential, but then she thought about how Sony's crying was linked to him transitioning in spaces in school. The therapist wondered if as a baby Sony hadn't cried as an infant because he had not realised his mother as separate and there was no need to call out for her for, after all, crying is an attempt to bring mother proximal. Perhaps Sony and his mother had struggled with the experience of separation. Moving house had not entirely registered, again, he had not acknowledged the move away. And now in school, all this was catching up with him. In school he was becoming acutely and painfully aware that separating and transitioning between spaces was a reality. And it was a reality for which he had no template.

Arguably, the first move away from mother is the blueprint that maps all those transitions to come. Perhaps and because that distance had yet to be travelled, Sony's capacity to move away from his mother was sorely compromised. On some level, in Sony's mind there was only one, not two, and there was no space in-between, he could only graft one habitat onto another. In an attempt to understand why the separation work had not taken place the therapist tried to understand what might have impeded this process. Sony's mother had experienced post-natal-depression and perhaps when the maternal eye is empty of feeling, as with a depressed or narcissistic mother, then the infant will encounter difficulties in finding a self. The self of the infant needs reflecting back. The infant might encounter the void of depression, only being left with the outline of the eye, the dark abyss of the pupil, the hole, the entrance to the mind's eye rather than the seeing, affirming eye that mirrors the infant's self. Or perhaps some infants encounter a mother so full of herself that there is no space to realise a concept of their own self. Narcissistic mothers who have not had sufficient self-other experiences themselves and have had to retreat inwards can struggle to behold their infant. So many children with a diagnosis of ASD avoid eye contact and struggle to see the other, not noticing peers, relating to staff as disembodied educators and facilitators, favouring technologies where there is a barrier to intimacy mediated through a screen, governed by a hard drive. It might be that the disproportionately high ratio of male to females diagnosed with ASD could be explained by the difficulty of the mother beholding the other that is a male baby, and an autistic retreat ensues. Female infants are more-self-than-other and, perhaps, a process of dual orientated narcissism (Salome, 1916) can better facilitate the development of self.

One of the first priorities for the primary school psychotherapist when starting to work in a school is to look at who might be struggling in nursery and foundation/reception. An investment during this time pays greater dividends later. School can be a baptism of fire when it comes to socialisation for both parent and child. From the get go children from school nursery have to manage the group. Attachment to, or detachment from, the group is something that staff use as an indicator of emotional wellbeing and social adjustment in the individual child. Parents who hitherto have had a quite a lot of control over what impacts upon their child, now have to contend with the challenges of classroom life. They might have to deal with a tearful child at the end of the day complaining about another child hurting them. They might have to receive their child's upset at being left out or unjustly reprimanded by the teacher when they believe another child was at fault. Their child might come home with language that is not used in the family and behaviours that have not been seen before. And whilst the school can be a useful repository for families to locate all things troubling, it is the first institution children inhabit and learn how to operate successfully with their peers and as such can be the first formal feedback a parent has about their child's behaviour. It might be the first formalised opportunity to compare and contrast their child's development with that of others. It might be that the counsellor's efforts are better placed supporting parents of troubled children for a contained parent is better able to contain a struggling child for it is they, after all, who are with the child when school has closed.

Working in a school with a child with a disorganised attachment: the girl who was her mother

Taylor was a first born nine-year-old-girl of dual heritage, Jamaican and White British. She was referred to the school counselling service principally, because she was disruptive in class, had little truck with authority and had struggled to make academic progress since Year Two. She was at times accusatory, leaving staff feeling vulnerable and open to possible complaint procedures. When the therapist undertook preliminary observations of Taylor in and around the school, she noticed that Taylor struggled to relate to her peers as equals. Taylor oscillated between behaving like a controlling parent and a dependant demanding infant. Separations between Taylor and her mother at the start of the day were emotionally charged and dramatic, often leaving both upset and dishevelled. Equally, there were fraught reunions as mum was informed by the class teacher of Taylor's behaviour during the day. This would lead to arguments, with mum getting angry with Taylor. Taylor would bury her face deep into her mum's belly, suck on her coat buttons and wrap her legs around her, or run after her as she walked away, jumping aboard her body as if the last lifeboat leaving a sinking ship. For her part, Mum would move between embracing Taylor, cupping her face in her hands, kissing her on the lips, opening her coat and engulfing her within it, to shouting at her and refusing contact. It was an intensely felt relationship.

Taylor's mum, Emma, had a reputation in the school as formidable and not someone to take on lightly. There had been some close calls in the playground with parental hostilities over-spilling and Emma had been involved in some of these. She was unable to adhere to the junior school rule of dropping Taylor off outside in the playground, routinely coming into the hallways, cloakroom, and classroom, volubly continuing her rather public parenting in one way or another. Teachers did not want to suggest to Emma that her daughter might need therapy and so the therapist left it for a while, as protocol was that school staff approached the parent prior to the therapist. Taylor then began petitioning the therapist to speak with her mother and so, finally, she decided she needed to broach the subject with Emma, whilst noticing that if adults were fearful of Emma it might not be a bad bet that Taylor was too.

The therapist found Emma in the playground at pick up time. Statuesque and broad she looked at the therapist's outstretched hand and ignored it. Taylor slipped behind a nearby wall on sight of the exchange and the therapist was left looking back at herself in Emma's reflective sunglasses, feeling somewhat diminished. Nevertheless, she introduced herself and after a brief explanation of concerns, Emma agreed to meet to think together about Taylor's situation. The first meeting together was marked by Emma's lively intelligence. Emma liked words, drawing on metaphor, delivering a poetic lace of language that, at times, made sense independent of word choice. In her mid-twenties, she spoke of her own troubled childhood with an absent father who wouldn't acknowledge her existence, and a mother who was an alcoholic with a series of abusive boyfriends. She died when Emma was nine years old due to a domestic violence incident, the perpetrator of which was never charged and Emma described as "walking around somewhere".

When Taylor was born, mum spoke of an immediate bond. She recounted a story of Taylor, a day or so after her birth, stopping breathing and it was her vigilance that brought her to the nurse's attention and potentially prevented her death. She also spoke of Taylor's younger brother being born dead and that she had begged the doctors to keep on resuscitating him. He too survived. The therapist felt that Emma was telling her that she had birthed both her children twice, once with her body and once with her will. She wondered if her will continued to parent them with the same hyper vigilance of life and death anxiety. She wondered if whether becoming a mother brought back the death of Emma's mother, not least as one of the last times she had been in a hospital was when at her mother's bedside as she lay dying. Emma spoke about memories of waiting for her mother to pick her up from school, she didn't come and she would walk home alone. Perhaps as Emma waited for her mother to come she wondered if she was dead or alive and each time she dropped off and picked up Taylor she had to relive this feeling. She parented Taylor as if the threat of death was ever present "walking around somewhere".

Emma's parenting was very public and the therapist wondered about this in relation to her mother's death which was very private, when actually she died as a result of domestic violence but there was no public inquiry, no trial, no jury, no verdict, no sentence. Taylor's father, Frazer, had been both present and absent throughout her childhood, and mum's relationship with him was, at times, volatile and teetered on the brink of separation but, equally, it had sustained itself over ten years and they seemed dedicated and loving toward one another. Emma had a good relationship with her mother-in-law and there were times when Frazer would go and stay with her when their relationship was under stress. He had been in prison around the time of Taylor's birth and due to being born outside of Britain his residency status was always a source of instability for the whole family. The therapist wondered about Frazer's capacity to attach and, more broadly, about the law and justice. As there had been some safeguarding concerns with Taylor the therapist scoped out the possibility that there might be some further safeguarding concerns, possibly coming from the therapy, and how that would play out in their relationship. Emma said she had nothing to hide. The therapist said that part of the problem with safeguarding now was that parents who were being called to account by school and Social Care might be the very same parents who, when they were children, were overlooked by school and Social Care and might have benefitted from their attention. This was a very difficult position to be in, both blamed and neglected. Both she and Frazer were on the receiving end of intersecting bureaucracies, which either seemed punitive or neglectful. The therapist wondered in what way social and political systems contributed to attachment anxieties expressed by Taylor.

The therapist also noticed that Taylor was approaching the age Emma was when she lost her mother and these sort of anniversarial aspects of family life across generations could be quite powerful and, perhaps, there were greater storms ahead. Emma spoke about Taylor being pubertal and described her as "producing". The therapist noted that puberty was a revolution of sorts and that the two colliding with one another might be even more incendiary. She noticed with Emma that she did not seem able to just drop Taylor off at school, something needed to be worked through at the threshold of separation each and every day. At the end of the assessment the therapist said to Emma that the things Emma had told her, had helped her make sense of Taylor's behaviour. Emma remained seated but pulled up to her full height then moved closer in to the therapist and said; "Are you trying to tell me that it's got something to do with me that Taylor is the way she is?" The therapist said that she thought Taylor's behaviour was something to do with how the family was now, and possibly shaped by the way things had been in the past. Emma said, "We'll think on then". They arranged a further meeting and continued to meet drawing on a parent partnership model whereby the focus was on the child but also how family history had shaped the parenting of the child.

The therapist formulated that both Taylor and Emma were conjoined, stuck together in a way that impinged upon Taylor developing an independent self. She thought that the glue was anxiety and fear. Emma was frightened, and frightening, and so was Taylor. The therapist further hypothesised that when either one tried to move away, the other was thrown into a state of either existential crisis or acute anxiety. Further, she felt the behaviours and history broadly fitted a disorganised attachment.

When therapy began with Taylor it was soon apparent that the end of the sessions were proving to be difficult with Taylor refusing to leave the room. It was only with a combination of cajoling and persuasion that a timely ending was managed, though it was also soon apparent that the journey back to the classroom was beginning to stretch with Taylor delaying her return to class by a series of distractions and detours. Further observations of Taylor in class highlighted that she could not remain in a state of independence or solitude for more than about fifteen seconds. She either targeted vulnerable children with a taunt or created a situation where the teacher would have to attend to her. It was also apparent how Taylor would adopt the gestures and behaviours of those around her, including her teachers, becoming didactic and directive with her peers and her teachers. On one occasion in the corridor, Taylor spoke to her therapist with a familiarity that didn't belong to a young child. The therapist asked Taylor; "who am I talking to, Taylor or Taylor's mum?". Taylor smiled and walked on. The therapist spoke with the teaching staff and asked what was known about Taylor, for instance; her favourite TV programme, what clothes she liked, hobbies, her interests and so forth, basically, who was she?

Bearing in mind how much staff time Taylor was taking up, everyone drew a blank. The therapist was left feeling that they needed to send out a search party for the most visible child in the school. One morning in breakfast club the therapist patted the chair next to her for Taylor to come over and talk to her, which Taylor did obligingly. Later on that morning when Taylor saw the therapist in the corridor, she sat down on a nearby bench and tapped on the space next to her inviting her therapist to sit down next to her. The therapist said; "You see when you pat the bench for me to come and sit with you, it is just like I did this morning when I wanted you to come and sit next to me in breakfast club? If I sit next to you now will that make you me and me you? Won't that be confusing? Maybe it is that I need to sit in your place to understand something better?"

In one of the early sessions Taylor was asked to draw a self-portrait. She drew a white female figure with hair and features that resembled Emma. When the therapist pointed out that she had a different colour hair and skin in the drawing, Taylor did not seem able to compute this. The therapist then fully realised the task ahead. She also anticipated that the boundary delineation needed to be tight in an effort to model a beginning and end. Several months into the individual sessions Taylor began to bluntly refuse to leave the therapy room. On one occasion she prevented her therapist from leaving the room. It was decided that if Taylor couldn't leave the room at the designated time then she was not allowed to come to the following session. After further repeats of refusal to leave followed by session forfeit, Taylor began to leave on time, and any additional amount of time it took to return to her classroom was deducted from her next session. Eventually, after nine months, Taylor was able to both leave the therapy room and the therapist was able to return Taylor to her class within the allotted boundary. Around this time the family Support Worker invited Taylor to draw a self-portrait and she drew a brown-skinned girl with braided hair, basically, she drew herself. A short while after this, Emma decided to pull Taylor out of therapy.

The situation with Taylor continued to feel volatile, with difficult behaviours in school and at home. A CAMHS referral was made. Social Care became involved for various reasons around safeguarding. Taylor ran out in front of a slow moving bus at one point shouting at it to run her over, at another point she pulled a knife on herself. Her behaviour was escalating at school and she was taken repeatedly to the calming room when felt to be unmanageable. Taylor was big for her age and quite strong so this often took the efforts of several staff members. The therapist tried to talk to staff about her behaviours in terms of whenever she was in a reflective space out of touch with others, she was exposed to very troubling thoughts and feelings and in order to avoid thinking and feeling these things, which were existential in nature, she would direct a drama in which many people were allocated a part. The therapist spoke to the Head Teacher about trying to minimise staff involvement in these by having only one person who was "in charge" and an "umbilical" member of staff who could alert other staff when necessary. On one occasion, after the implementation of this system, the therapist found Taylor wondering around the school (with one staff member at a discreet distance). Taylor appeared disorientated and said to the therapist, "Are you looking for me?" The therapist said; "No, but I think you are". Taylor then went back to her classroom and remained settled for the rest of the day.

The culture of the school was that staff pulled together and were very supportive of one another. However, staff were split on the matter of Taylor. Some thought she needed more understanding, others thought she had pushed too far and was long overdue a permanent exclusion. Some felt threatened by Taylor, while others didn't. For a reasonably harmonious team the subject of Taylor would bring a hitherto unseen heat to exchanges between staff. The therapist thought the split was a manifestation of what was happening between Taylor and Emma but she also felt that Taylor needed to have clear communications about what was and wasn't acceptable, and there would come a time when everyone's patience ran out. Taylor needed to understand what "giving up" and "letting go" looked and felt like. The relationship between Taylor and her mother had a relentless quality to it and even if she did, at times, feel like running away Emma would not have given up on Taylor.

The therapist imagined them both in heated, entangled exchange when Emma was collecting her pension with Taylor never having left home.

The other problem was that whenever Taylor had behaved in an unacceptable way that was sustained, Emma would be called to come and collect her. As the therapist was trying to work with Emma not to come into the school building at all, and to try to have some faith and trust that the world could be a benign place and keep Taylor safe, the two "systems", therapeutic and educational, were working in understandable opposition to one another. So whenever Taylor felt anxious about whether she existed or not, she would create a scene which led to her mother coming in. On the one hand this offered her reassurance for she was her mother and her mother appearing meant she had found herself on some level. On the other hand her mother was furious with her so this exacerbated her fears. Further, this action by the school just confirmed Emma's world view that the only world in which Taylor could feel safe was hers. The therapist conceded that perhaps Taylor (and Emma) would benefit from a school that was able to keep them separate until it came to home time. After further struggles, which resulted in Taylor threatening the safety of other children, the school had to exclude Taylor and she moved to a special school that was in a better position to manage their separation. CAMHS also withdrew at this point, having completed their eight session input focusing on Taylor's anger and suggesting strategies to manage this.

In spite of the school move the therapist continued working with Emma and tried to unpick situations where things between Emma and Taylor had become furious and threatening. Each time it was possible to construe these times in terms of a disorganised attachment. Emma became increasingly able to identify the triggers of a "not-me-who-is-me?" crisis, and when things had calmed between the two she was able to bring this thinking to Taylor. Emma sought an assessment with a paediatrician and Taylor was diagnosed with ADHD although medication was declined by Emma. Eventually Taylor was returned to a mainstream school and she settled reasonably well. Social Care withdrew from the family feeling that their work was done. The therapist attended the multi-agency meeting where this news was delivered to Emma and she received it as something akin to a graduation certificate.

Nearing the end of Year Six, and in preparation for increased independence of secondary school, a residential trip was planned. The therapist and Emma anticipated that Taylor might sabotage this by behaving in a challenging way. She did. However Emma was able to stand firm, hold on to her own anxieties and bear the prospect of Taylor sleeping away from her for the first time. The trip was managed with a great deal of anxiety on both their parts but on the way home Taylor refused to put her seat belt on. Staff had to stand next to her, holding onto the seat belt for the journey home. Clearly, the transition back home needed to express the attachment anxiety that Taylor felt.

So what are we to make of all of this? In Taylor's case, we might wonder if there was some unmetabolised trauma which had been transmitted across generations, for example her mother's own distressing history, with attachment and separation traumas which were now being replayed with Taylor. Research tells us that where we have unresolved grief, it can become unconsciously buried exerting greater psychological disturbance in subsequent generations (Fonagy 1999; Kestenberg, 1982; Winship & Knowles, 1997). Specifically in Taylor's case, Taylor's mother had lost her own mother at a young age, and so there appeared to be elements of the loss replayed in Taylor's anxiety, and in particular enacted in the difficulties she faced in being on her own, and in managing the end of each session. It would appear more than just mere coincidence that the age when Taylor began therapy was the same age that her mother lost her own mother. Perhaps the transgenerational transmission of trauma on this occasion found some receptivity to mending it.

Almost inevitably Taylor's birth and early life had been a time of great anxiety and her mothering would have been infused with this anxiety and unresolved grief. The arms, the mind, the gaze, the smile, the frown, the voice, the touch, the smell, the fear all would have conveyed to Taylor that the nursery was filled with ghosts and demons. Main and Hesse (1990) talk about the parent who is frightened when the infant is distressed and how fear can be a central mechanism in the transmission of unresolved transgenerational trauma. One might speculate that there was little room for Taylor's nascent self to flourish, their attachment was characterised by an adhesive attachment, so there no space for a separate self to emerge. The same trauma source might also explain why Taylor was so disruptive in class inasmuch as her noisiness and intruding into the space of other children was a defence against solitariness which she experienced as distressing. As a consequence Taylor became frightened and needed the continuous holding presence of others. Taylor needed to keep a constant line between herself and others, including her teachers and peers, and then also her therapist who she could not let go of at the end of a session. Taylor was "drawing a line" between herself and others and these were probably felt to be lifelines that stopped her from falling forever. These lines came to resemble something of a spider's web; a matrix or network of web-lifelines that were attempts to fix herself to others around her, albeit often antagonistically. Taylor had worked out that by making someone irritated, exasperated or angry with her, achieved a greater lifeline fix. During the school day, these lifelines held her until her mum returned to collect her at the end of the day.

We might think of these types of anxious and disorganised attachments that serve a function for young children before their parents return. These attachment patterns are probably more commonly played out with teachers in their role as *loco parentis* than are ordinarily recognised. It was clear from the outset that there were attachment difficulties between mother and Taylor that resembled the features of "disorganised attachment" (Main & Solomon, 1986) such as unresolved trauma, the uncertainty of parental responses and fear of the parent. Taylor's controlling behaviours were possibly attempts to ameliorate uncertainty (George & Solomon, 1996; Lyons-Ruth, 1996). On occasions when Mum and Taylor were reunited they sometimes appeared conjoined, a sort of conjoined psyche, almost Siamese in character. Of course a strong mother and daughter bond is healthy, but in Mum and Taylor's case there was an "adhesion" between them which brings to mind a sort of less healthy "stickiness" that Bick (1968) talked about. Bick identified fear unmodulated by containment as central and she paid particular attention to how the infant makes use of the body to try to manage this.

Meltzer (1974) developed this idea in his work on "adhesive identification". Meltzer was interested in autistic phenomena and "surface seeking children" who, he argued, did not understand internal spaces. This idea seemed to fit Taylor insofar as she seemed to attack or deny external and transitional space, an example of this being the occasions when Taylor would run at staff and mum trying to cling on. Her collapsing the space between school and the counselling service when she refused to transition between therapy room and classroom and staff from the counselling service and school had to interface in a way they hadn't previously, and her refusal to leave the therapy room. The situation with Taylor called for a different approach from the therapist. She became more drawn in to thinking about how the school managed behaviours than she had done previously. Emma almost operated like a staff member, as she was such a fixture in the school she took to commenting on other children's behaviours and occasionally disciplining them. Taylor also took on the role of teacher reprimanding other children at times. Staff were repeatedly heard to say, "I'm the adult, you're the child." Boundaries were stretched and collapsed. Staff feared loss of control and, at times, became bewildered and disorientated. Order needed reinstating and this seemed to draw the entire infrastructure of statutory care and provision. From teaching assistants, to educational psychologists, to therapists, to paediatricians, to social workers, to police, to assert a model not only of containment but something alluding to transgenerational justice.

The situation of working with the mother–child couple in this case gives some scope to the possibilities of dual intervention in the setting of the primary school therapy service. A therapeutic intervention working with both parent and child offers, on the one hand, a place for some exploratory work with mother and on the other hand a creative therapy opportunity with the child. In this case, the joint approach was a chance to estimate the intensity of attachment disruption between Taylor and her mother, and thereafter the potential for therapy to offer a new synthesis. As Mother and Taylor were able to engage in the therapeutic process, letting go of each other without calamity, Mother was able to move to a new stage of letting go of her own mother. She was able to recognise that she had given birth to another and that she needed to mourn her loss of mothering and allow Taylor to have something she never had, a sober, attentive, dedicated mother who not only lived for her child, but more importantly lived.

CHAPTER FOUR

On knowing—containment and thinking

Brief

The term "containment" in mental health and psychiatric taxonomy usually has a pejorative undertow summoning up ideas of incarceration, restraint, and case management. This chapter considers containment as a psychological event, and begins with a detailed case account illustrating aspects of containment during the course of working with a mother–daughter. We review how "containment" has come to be a subject of common parlance in psychoanalytic theory and practice tracing the emergence of the concept from its origins in passing references to the term in the 1950s, to its theoretical anchoring by Wilfred Bion in 1962 with his model of the "container" and the "contained". We make a case for thinking about two types of containment; (i) endoskeletal and (ii) exoskeletal, the former referring to the inside experience of mother's containment, the latter belonging to a more externally derived experience of paternal containment. We consider containment as a transmodal essential ingredient of the therapeutic encounter, and a useful concept for understanding the alliance between the therapist and client across all the modes of talking therapy.

Case study

Five-year-old Bella was diagnosed with autistic spectrum disorder (ASD) at eighteen months. In her second term in nursery she was referred to the counselling service through the family support worker, who was concerned as to the vulnerability of the whole family. The therapist met with mother, Sam, and decided to work with her using more of a psycho-educational model, looking at parenting but also looking at Sam's early life and how this might have shaped the person and parent she had become. Alongside this the therapist also observed Bella on an ongoing basis in the classroom with a view to working with her on a one-to-one basis at a later date. Further, the therapist worked closely with the family support worker, the classroom teaching assistant (TA), and teacher. The therapist and Sam met once a week for fifty minutes during term time.

One of the main concerns for the teachers was that Bella would not go to the toilet at school, spending much of her day jiggling around as if desperate to do so. She would wait until she was collected by her mother, and when they returned home, it was only then that Bella would; "let go", as Sam put it. The therapist wondered what it might be that Bella did not want to let go of, or what it was that she wanted to hold on to? Certainly Mum seemed anxious about letting go of Bella at drop off time, yet Bella would drift off as if there had been no separation at all. The therapist wondered if the struggle to "let go" was symbolic, perhaps a failure to mourn. What was it that the held wee represented? Did Bella feel it to be part of herself and therefore, letting it leave her body would be experienced as some sort of psychological haemorrhaging of "self"?

Bella had a poor appetite, occasionally she would pick at solid food but, largely, she would eat yoghurts and protein drinks prescribed by the health visitor. As she moved between the second to sixth centile there were concerns about her weight. She was often constipated and would go for days without pooing. Opening her bowels was a painful experience. Bella would scream and would express fear at the prospect of her poo coming. Again, the therapist tried to understand this in terms of Bella experiencing her faeces as something alien to her, perhaps something that alerted her to an inside, or perhaps the experience of a part of her falling out. It seemed, for Bella, as if inside and outside spaces were not clearly delineated.

Bella was the last of seven children, all of whom had a diagnosis of ASD with the eldest two in kinship care. Bella was small boned with fine auburn hair and pale, almost translucent, skin. Her eyes were mostly cast down, and she would only meet the gaze of others if requested. Sometimes it seemed to be a burden for Bella to keep her eyes open. Sam said that Bella would always be her baby and she was sad that she would be her last. Sam saw little prospect of things changing for Bella and the therapist wondered if, along with the part of Sam that wanted Bella to follow a conventional developmental trajectory, there was a part of Sam that didn't really want Bella to grow up and become independent.

Over a series of initial observations, the therapist noticed that Bella did not engage with her peers, she presented as if in a world of her own, remote, unpopulated, and whispered. However, Bella demonstrated an alert intelligence and was keenly engaged with classroom work, even if she did not appear to make contact with the teacher. She seemed to excel at mind-to-mind work, for instance she could answer mathematical questions, but when it came to instructions for social engagement, Bella would retreat into herself. Her peers intuited her otherness, accepting her difference with equanimity, at times being expressly maternal toward her, stroking her hair, patting her head, cooing. If she was satisfied with something she had achieved she would flap her hands excitedly. The therapist wondered if Bella somehow needed feelings to be shaken from her body as if they had no place within, almost as if she was without internal space to contain them. Then she would hop on one foot as if unearthed by the experience of feeling. She would pull up her knees really high as if the floor were scorched, as if her feeling were something that she could not easily stand.

Mum had a childlike quality about her. She would sit on the chair in the therapist's room with her legs dangling, twiddling her thumbs, and smiling. The therapist went looking for Sam beyond the caricature and quickly found an alert mind. Sam recounted a deeply troubled and acutely deprived childhood, which would almost certainly have instigated care proceedings in contemporary child protection practice. Sam was brought up in considerable poverty by a mother who came from an itinerant family and had significant learning and mental health difficulties. Sam estimated her mother's mental age to be seven or eight. Her father was a violent alcoholic and he too had a psychiatric profile, but on the rare occasion he was sober she had some fond memories of him. Both parents had met when sectioned under the Mental Health Act.

Sam referred to herself as "probably autistic". She no longer felt her way through life and had cried only once in adult life, as far as she could remember. When the therapist talked to Sam about her childhood, Sam chimed, "The past is the past." "Sometimes the past is the present," the therapist replied whilst acknowledging how necessary it can be to bracket off experience sometimes. The therapist asked Sam if she thought the work they were doing together could bear both the past and present being in the room at the same time. Sam said she willing to give it a try.

Sam and her husband tried their best to create the childhood for their children that she would have wished for herself. She spoke of not wanting to upset her children and so rarely challenged them, rather she tried her best to provide them with what they wanted. She said she would not allow herself to get angry with them. The therapist wondered how creating an "idyllic" home life prepared her children for a life so often filled with frustration and disappointment. Sam agreed that life "outside" was far from ideal; they had moved multiple times due to complaints from the neighbours about noise and even though a part of her wanted to keep her children in a bubble, she said she wanted them to go out into the big wide world. The therapist, again, thought of this in terms of a failure to mourn.

Sam spoke of her pregnancy with Bella as stressful, becoming unwell, being hospitalised, and given a series of antibiotics and steroids. In the latter stages of her pregnancy she became preoccupied with a noise, percussive and insistent, coming from what she believed to be the walls of her house, or possibly the neighbours. Once she went looking for the noise in a nearby bush. The therapist wondered if the noise was similar to that of a heartbeat and Sam agreed that it was. The therapist wondered whether Sam was looking outside of herself for something that was within, that is, Bella's heartbeat or perhaps her own.

Sam said that she thought she had been destined to produce autistic children. The therapist asked her how that made her feel about the inside of her body while she was gestating her babies. Maybe it wasn't possible to think about the inside of her? Maybe it hadn't been possible to connect with the inside and it needed to be projected outside to manage the experience of being full with another, like the heartbeat that was in the bush? She had lost her first two children and the following four were in receipt of a diagnosis by the time she was pregnant with Bella. Perhaps it just hadn't been possible to think about Bella when she was inside her. Again there seemed to be a struggle to delineate interior and exterior space, some breakdown in containment.

Sam had developed pre-eclampsia towards the end of the pregnancy and after going two weeks overdue she was induced. Labour did not progress and just as they were preparing Sam for an emergency C-section Sam said that Bella appeared. Her body had not registered the birth; Bella was "just there". Sam described having "a huge connection" when Bella was born and she was "special". Bella was a poor feeder, and she would choke regularly. The therapist made a connection between Bella's ongoing struggle to ingest and digest and her struggle to expel. She also noticed that perhaps Bella hadn't quite been birthed.

Bella was often unwell and was unable to go for any sustained period maintaining her health. Sam spoke of realising fairly quickly that all was not well with Bella. She spoke of her being set off by particular sounds such as Sellotape and the closing of curtains. The therapist wondered about the noises in the delivery suite. The tape readying for the epidural; the sudden pulling of the curtains around Sam's bed. Bella would roll into curtains and wrap herself up so Sam could not see her. The therapist wondered what Sam's gaze was like? As Sam had chosen to retreat from feeling, did her eyes convey an absence? Apparently Bella would suck on the knuckles of crossed fingers. The therapist tried this herself and concluded that it was jarring, and that unlike sucking a thumb, which found an easy partnership with the concave roof of the mouth, Bella's comforter was closer to a fist. Nevertheless this was Bella's version of self-soothing however difficult it was for her to accommodate. Did she not grasp the interiority of her mouth?

Sam hoarded household goods and was in an almost perpetual cycle of buying and selling cars, furniture, and technical equipment online. This seemed to entail a dynamic loop of winning and losing bids, married with anticipation of owning and disowning materials. The therapist wondered if this cycle was a way of working through holding onto and letting go of. Sam spoke of hoping that she could buy the perfect life, the happy home and if, say, the sofa became soiled it had to be sold on and replaced with a "perfect" one. When this was discussed with the therapist, she agreed that to look upon a damaged and soiled object was something of a concrete representation or reminder of how damaged and soiled she herself felt.

Sam said she didn't trust anyone and that if friends or acquaintances troubled her too much she could just cut them from her life. The therapist wondered what her experiences might mean for their relationship. The therapist put to Sam that she might see her therapy as part of social care surveillance, as previously social care professionals had intervened to try to remove her first two children. Sam had spoken of the social workers pretending to be concerned about her but they had an ulterior motive. Perhaps Sam experienced the therapist as someone pretending to be interested? The therapist suggested they put the notion of trust to one side as she couldn't expect someone who had been so terribly let down by others to trust her. She reminded Sam that she was, of course, in charge of what she brought to the session and she was at liberty to come or not and, as it transpired, Sam only ever missed one session.

As the work progressed the therapist found herself, on a couple of occasions, welling up with tears as Sam gave a vivid but emotionless account of distressing events in her childhood. She wondered with Sam whose upset she was feeling, and said that it didn't seem to have been safe to have feelings in Sam's childhood as it made her too vulnerable. She wondered how having her feelings locked up in a far-away place impacted upon Bella and her siblings. For, however troubling and messy feelings are, they allow us to engage with, and connect to others in a meaningful way. "When we feel, we are alive," the therapist offered to Sam, who agreed but said she preferred to stay away from feelings as they were "too difficult". The therapist understood that being dead to feeling might preserve the self from being overwhelmed by some terrible experiences but suggested to Sam that she stay curious about what was happening with the feeling states of the children at home. That she might make guesses as to what their underlying feelings might be and to see if they could be put into words. As the weeks progressed Sam tried her very best to do just that.

Sam was prepared to take suggestions on board if they made sense to her. Her own mother struggled to think. Her father struggled to stay conscious. All her birth family could not bear to feel and her current family could not think about feeling. Given the time and resources available, the therapist wasn't sure if participating in a process that encouraged a dismantling of defences against feeling was the primary objective. Instead she prioritised thinking about feeling. There were some fundamentals of family functioning that needed addressing first, their social isolation in particular,was pressing. In order to open up the possibility of greater connectedness to others the therapist highlighted any opportunities for Sam to introduce self/other moments into the family.

Bella had been refusing to sleep in her own room and wedged herself between both her parents, not in a "spooning" way, more that the three formed a wonky "H". This reminded the therapist of the shape Bella's knuckles would make as she sucked on them and, more generally, about the autistic shapes of which Tustin (1984) talks of. Although this significantly disrupted Sam's sleep, she could not bear the upset that ensued if she tried to return Bella to her bed. The therapist wondered if Sam might be better able to bear the upset of her children when she was better able to bear her own upset, that there might be a mutuality in the arrangement. She wondered whether when Sam was ready to let go of Bella, Bella would find her way to her own bed.

Some months into working with Sam, the therapist suggested that both she and Sam go and collect Bella from class and introduce her to the therapy room with a view to observing how they both interacted. This would be quite a break to Bella's routine, which was that Sam would drop her off in the morning and collect her at lunchtime. So the therapist and Sam duly went to collect Bella from nursery. She was engrossed in an activity and the teacher called her from it, informing her that the therapist and mummy had come to collect her. She turned from what she was doing and stared across at her mother in a state of non-recognition. Sam said, "Hello, Bella, are you coming with me?" Bella stared blankly at Sam for some time then turned back to the activity she was doing. The therapist observed that it was as if the space between them in the room was simply not navigable, Bella could not countenance that her mother was over there and she was over here, so to speak. It was almost as if there was an abyss between Bella and her mother and if she were to take one step towards her mother she might fall over some unseen precipice.

Sam was taken aback and a little hurt by the exchange until the therapist shared this thought with her. The therapist said that perhaps Bella did not think that she and Sam were separate, they were conjoined and that she simply could not conceive of her in a different space to her so she turned as if it hadn't happened. She flagged up with Sam that perhaps she and Bella adopted the same defence mechanism: both behaved as if the painful, difficult things hadn't happened. Perhaps neither of them, on some level, had acknowledged that Bella had been birthed. The therapist started to think of Bella as part pre-born, part savant and set about spending time with her when she began in reception class after the summer break. She spoke with the TA about some of her thinking, which chimed with that of the TA, and they began a working collaboration in relation to Bella.

Over the following few months several significant developmental moments began to unfold. Bella's language was very limited and almost wholly adhesive. Mostly should would just say "yes" to whatever people said to her or she would echo the last word of the sentence as if the significant communication for Bella was that something had come to an end and she needed to hold onto this. One day the therapist sat next to Bella in class and started to draw around her own hand. Bella became interested in what she was doing and the therapist invited Bella to lay her hand flat on the paper so that she could draw around it. Bella did so, placing her hand a short distance from the therapist's hand outline, and the therapist drew around her hand. Bella became very excited by this and gestured for the therapist to do it again, and again, and again, by placing her hand on different spaces on the paper. The following week the therapist was crossing the hall and she saw Bella and waved. Bella waved back. Later that week they crossed paths again and Bella said, "Hello, Sarah." She had never heard Bella say two consecutive words, she hadn't seen her look up for contact that wasn't instigated by another, and she hadn't known her to reach out with a communication that was not a repetition of what another had said. Was it that Bella having found a part of herself, enabled her to reach out to others?

The therapist thought the time might be right to invite Bella into the therapy room. In their first session, which lasted a few minutes before Bella moved to return to class, she held the therapist's hand as they walked from class to the room. When she entered she went straight to the doll's house and picked up the small ceramic toilet. The therapist said, "You need to talk to me about the wee-wee?" The following week she did the same thing and, as she was clearly in need of the toilet, the therapist asked if Bella wanted to go for a wee-wee. She said "yes" and so the therapist took her to the toilet area but Bella did not go to the toilet and so they returned to the room. This went on for several weeks. The therapist felt that Bella might be interested in letting go of mum and that in order to do that mum needed to be able to let go of Bella. The therapist continued to talk with Sam about her childhood along with Bella's toileting. Bella had more recently had a few "accidents"; wetting herself both at school and then on occasions as soon as she got into the car after school. The therapist spoke to Sam about the possibility of not framing these as accidents but celebrating the fact that she was able to let go without recourse to the nappy. Sam stopped using the disappointed face and the word "accident", as did school staff.

Bella's language started developing. Sam came to see the therapist one morning remarking that Bella had actually said a whole sentence. The sentence was, "Going to chop your face out." Sam was taken aback and the therapist wondered with her what this might mean. Whilst the therapist noted that the sentence seemed to indicate a separateness between the two, albeit fleetingly, as Bella was going to do something to Sam, it was difficult not to think of this as an attack not only on Sam's face, but also on Sam herself. What was it that Sam's face expressed, or didn't express, that Bella felt the need to chop out? If her face was chopped out, what would it look like and would this more accurately represent Bella's experience? Was it an attempt to see what lay beneath? The chopping out of her mum's face would certainly expose some sort of interior, as opposed to a surface. Further, the threat offered up an alternative to the "happy" home and family environment that Sam was so keen to preserve. There would certainly be some strength of feeling expressed if Bella had chopped out Sam's face.

The therapist started to notice Bella in the lunch hall. She observed how she didn't chop her food or bite into it with any conviction, preferring to scrape the surface of it. She suggested to Sam that she might buy some play dough or plasticine and encourage Bella to cut it up. She also suggested encouraging Bella to bite through food, say a cube of chocolate or an apple, and see if she could find the imprint of her teeth. The following week Sam reported that Bella had asked for a knife to chop up the jelly she was eating. Little by little, over the following months, the range of foods Bella was prepared to eat extended. Also, perhaps some of Bella's aggression found its way into the bite and cut of ordinary life and play.

Sam reported that Bella had started to use another name at home so she was Bella at school and Ellie at home. The therapist wondered if she needed two identities to help her begin to imagine her separateness from mother. The therapist thought that Bella might be looking for a separate self, an "I" which she could take into relationships with peers, instead of being conjoined with her mother. She ventured that with increasing independence for Sam, Bella might also experience independence, a separate self. The following week Sam relayed that Bella had gone into the fridge and taken out two sachets of yoghurt and handed one to Sam and said, "It's for you." Sam, quite rightly, identified this as a significant moment. Perhaps Bella was wakening to the idea that they were two.

The therapist continued to work with mother looking at her struggle to let go of Bella. But also at her feelings of superiority and inferiority, her contempt for those who thought she was stupid, her capacity to cut loose from feelings and people. Sam was able to speak further of some of the hurts and humiliations she had endured in her childhood. She asked, "Why would my mother visit such cruelties upon me? Why am I numb to feeling?" She became increasingly interested in why she was the way she was and the impact this had on her children. Slowly, Sam's hoarding habits changed, the contents of the garage had halved and she had lived with the same sofa for several weeks, which was a record.

The therapist and Sam spoke about how her special relationship with Bella was impacting upon her relationship with her other daughter who was expressing intense anger. The therapist suggested that this exclusive relationship must be excluding for the other children and perhaps some of the older sister's anger was related to this exclusion. Bella finally started to sleep in her own room and this created more space for Sam's relationship with Bella's sister. The therapist, worked with the family support worker to form a cooking group and Sam attended this, finding a bond with one other mother in particular. After a year of working together, Sam reported to the therapist that she was feeling much more confident in her ability to parent and manage life and also reported that she was more at ease allowing her husband to go to work, and not feeling the need to control him as she had done previously. Bella was becoming a more integrated member of the class. She was observant of class rules and mores and, at times, reinforced them. In particular, she seemed to have a connection with another boy in the class with a diagnosis of autism. Bella was also bringing some of her upset into school, usually in relation to her will and the expression of her individuality being thwarted such as refusing to wear school uniform. The TA battled these times out with her with great fortitude. At these times Bella cried and wailed and it seemed as if much working through was taking place. The one remaining behaviour, identified from the outset, was that Bella was still not toileting at school.

One day the therapist showed Bella a 3-D model of the human body, a teaching aid used for a biology lesson. She explained to Bella the journey of food and drink and the processes they were subject to, and that the food and drink came out as wee and poo. The therapist wondered with Bella about her struggle to let go of her wee and wondered if it was about mummy, and letting go of mummy in some way. Bella listened and watched with a keen interest and went on her way. The very next day when the therapist was at work sitting in her office, feeling a little despondent about one thing and another, she heard a knock at her door. She peered out to see a beaming TA holding Bella's hand. She said they had something to show her and they all walked to the toilets together. Bella had done a wee in the toilet. Delight all round. They flushed the toilet and waved bye-bye. Back at the therapist's office Bella had some chocolate. She bit through it, showed the therapist her teeth marks and said, "This is truly delicious," as she swallowed the remaining half. From that point on, with the occasional "accident" here and there, Bella toileted at school.

After the summer break Sam and the therapist met for a catch up. Sam told the therapist that she went to visit her mother for the first time in nineteen years. This was also the first time she had ever left her children overnight. Sam spent three days in the company of her mother and sister. Sam cooked tea for them and generally looked after them. One evening her sister collapsed sobbing onto her mother's lap and cried because she could never have what Sam had. Sam said she felt something in the pit of her stomach. She felt for her sister and that there was nothing she could do or buy to make her sister's situation better. The therapist acknowledged what an important moment this was for all three of them. Perhaps what Sam felt in the pit of her stomach was a feeling. Maybe the feeling was sadness for the despair of another. The therapist wondered that when one is able to feel empathy with another it is because they can bear to feel sad for what they have lost or have never had. Sam spoke of letting go and forgiving. The therapist said that letting go and mourning loss had felt almost impossible when they first met. She noticed how important the notion of letting go and grieving were even if they were fleeting, but now Sam was beginning to manage and contain these feelings.

Thinking about containment

During the one year and a term that the work took place with Sam and Bella, the therapist tried to model the type of containment that might be offered by a thoughtful mother who was curious about what was happening with her offspring. The idea of containment can be seen as threaded throughout the case account; from the idea of the body as container of Bella's biological waste, through to the challenge for Sam of holding on to feelings, containing them in her mind, and then speaking of them. The therapist tried to help Sam contain the thoughts and be curious about what her children were feeling. We might also notice the template for the model of containment in Bella's early fist sucking activities, the mouth is the container and her fist is the contained object. The therapist worked with the hypothesis that Bella's difficulties in eating pointed to an injured container–contained relationship, that is, Sam had found it difficult to contain Bella emotionally, and this would manifest in Bella's difficulties.

So in the case study we see the way in which the therapist worked towards helping Sam develop the emotional capacity to hold feelings in mind, containment as a mental process. If one has an ear for the word "containment", you might find yourself struck by the frequency of the use of the word, not only by counsellors and psychotherapists, but by a range of mental health professionals. For example, a psychotherapy student on her first placement complained that her six-year-old client was "difficult to contain because he was climbing on the table and running around the therapy room". The placement supervisor explored the meaning of the use of the word "contain". It turned out that there were at least two things that the word was seeking to convey; first, the trainee's experience of sitting with her own nervous energy, and second, the challenge of finding a way to manage and calm the client safely within the walls of the room. It was also noted that in using the word, the student was not cognisant of the theories of Bion.

The term containment is usually deployed within the orbit of an experience of a process of first, emotionally holding the client in mind and second, the idea of doing containment. The idea of doing containment probably overlaps in the margins between containment as a facet of mental process aligned with emotional labour, and then the way in which the term can be used interchangeably with the notion of managing a difficult situation, physical containment for instance is a term by front-line professional who might be de-escalating a social situation such as crowd control. The idea of containment in the psychological and emotional sense of the word, should be drawn from the ordinary human task of relating to another in distress, for instance as a mother contains her baby. In order to build a theory of containment we need to pay heed to how containment has been defined because if we have a theoretical anchor we can observe it in practice, thereafter we can research it and finally we can modify and then teach it as a concept. Hopefully we can do all of these things with a concept like containment, without killing its obvious natural utility.

Notably the increase in the use of the term containment can be seen in the number of academic papers that have made reference to the concept especially in psychoanalytic literature. For example in a search of the *International Journal of Psychoanalysis* we compared the use of the term "containment" with the use of the word "transference". First, we counted all the papers in the *International Journal of Psychoanalysis* where the paper had made mention of the term "containment", and then we repeated the same search for the term "transference". We then clustered these papers across a decade. The table below summarises our findings:

	Before 1950	1950– 1959	1960– 1969	1970– 1979	1980– 1989	1990– 1999	2000– 2009	2010– 2016
Containment	0	4	8	18	39	136	214	134
Transference	81	75	486	381	440	919	961	553

The search confirmed that from 1980 there has been a steady increase in the number of articles using the term containment with a sharp rise from 1990. In the 1970s the ratio of papers talking about containment compared to transference was 1:21 but since 2000 this ratio has shrunk to 1:5. We have not looked in detail at all of the papers, so it is not possible to comment on the frequency of mentions within the papers. Nonetheless, the search does point to the evolution of a concept. While containment has some way to go before it is considered as central to clinical practice as the concept of transference, we can argue that it has come to be something of an essential ingredient of psychotherapy.

The evolution of a concept

The term "containment" as a theoretical concept is usually attributed to Wilfred Bion (1959). However, presentiments of the process of conceptualisation were expressed prior to Bion. We might say that the concept of containment was a good idea looking for a theorist, a thought looking for a thinker we might say. The earliest mention of "containment" in the literature is in 1950 by William Pious who referred to the developmental task of the "containment of aggression" (1950, p. 282) by a mother in the first few months of an infant's life. Pious (1950) argued that a faulty maternal engagement might be characterised by a failure to adequately "bind aggression" (p. 282), resulting in the unsatisfactory development of the infant's superego. Instead of being able to experience aggression as contained, so Pious continues, the infant develops in an emotional vacuum and the longer-term consequences might be a schizophrenic-type uncanny hush or sinister stillness.

Moloney (1954) likewise deployed the term "containment" to describe the emotional management of aggressive urges, only this this time with specific reference to a client who had uncontrollable vomiting. Moloney considered the client as having suffered a loss of "self-containment" (p. 148), which had led to uncontrolled body discharges, and the vomiting was an expression of rage. In a paper the following year, Solomon situated nail-biting as a behaviour that deployed as way of containing aggression:

> the process of nail biting can be looked upon as an integrated act of release of aggression, denial and self-punishment by biting at the claws ... a medium for containment or assistance in establishing other integrative masteries in the face of ... tension-provoking situations. (Solomon, 1955, p. 394)

Notably, all three of these papers were from North America, and not one made any reference to Melanie Klein or the work that was happening in the British school of objects relations. Maloney and Solomon would seem to have a something of a concept of self-containment as mental process manifest with somatic presentation. Pious, and to some extent Moloney, have an idea that emotional containment might be considered in terms of a maternal task or a manifestation of maternal engagement, both ideas which resemble the arena of theory that moves towards Klein's emphasis of exploring the emotional turbulence between mother and infant. The idea of containment between subjects also foreshadows the way in which Bion would unfold the idea. Taken together, the three presentiment papers on "containment" could be said to suggest an ideological base consonant with the British school of object relations, though independently conceived. That is, although there is only a brief mention of the idea of containment in the North American papers, there is alignment in as far as the concept begins to illustrate the psychic mechanism of emotional management, usually in the context of dealing with aggressive or hostile impulses.

When Bion and other British Kleinian group colleagues began to use the term, the debate was invigorated similarly around the way in which a mother dealt with the most primitive anxieties and aggressions of an infant. The idea of containment suggested a new way of understanding the prototype of early emotional exchange. It was Herbert Rosenfeld (1952), another of Klein's protégés, who was the first to allude to the concept of containment in a clinical vignette when he discussed the nature of a patient's projection referring to what was "contained inside" the projection. But it was Bion who made a sustained effort to develop a distinct theory of containment, though before we describe Bion's theory, it is necessary to first summarise another key concept, that of projective identification (PI) because it is from the scaffolding of PI that Bion built his theory of containment.

Although there are debates that have elaborated the theory of projective identification, it is generally agreed that the concept refers us to the way in which early emotional exchange happens between mother and infant, and of course understanding this process is an essential ingredient of making sense of the therapist client exchange. In the first instance, Klein (1946) surmised that the infant was able to "split off" aspects of their emotional state, particularly those experiences that were felt to be injurious. These negative feeling states would be projected outwards and then taken in (introjected) by the concerned other, usually mother in the first place. Klein coined the term "projective identification" to define this process of emotional communication. Klein argued that usually the infant's mother was readily able to absorb the communications, and that this communication took place from birth onwards and certainly long before baby was able to use words to articulate felt emotional states.

The idea gained currency among Klein's students and then later her colleagues and as the theory was elaborated, Klein's followers began to apply the idea to a range of unconscious pathways of communication. Some of Klein's followers, especially Bion and Rosenfeld, noted that projective identification was particularly helpful when trying to understand more extreme emotional states such as psychosis where the usual mechanisms of conscious communication were defeated by distress acuity.

As Klein had made the controversial assertion that there was an early developmental phase in infancy called the paranoid-schizoid stage, her followers working with psychotic clients were starting to see how this idea could be a recurring process later in life. In other words, for those who got stuck at the paranoid-schizoid level, a lifetime of schizophrenia might await. In a sense, it was the disturbed mind of the psychotic adult that could throw further light on the speculations about the mind of an infant and young child that Klein had been trying to describe.

Bion's (1967, 1970) work with schizophrenic patients led him to formulate hypotheses in relation to hallucinations and delusions which he saw as evidence of "split off" aspects of the mind much in the same way that Klein had speculated about the splitting-off of emotions in infancy. In other words, Bion thought that delusions and hallucinations were fragments of imagination that might appear to be real to the individual suffering from psychosis. These split off aspects of mind returned mostly as unwelcomed "bizarre objects". Bion suggested that the term "splitting" be reserved for phenomena presented only in the most severely disturbed patients and that "dissociation" referred to the more gentle process of demarcation between split off aspects of the mind. He also suggested that the psychotic personality used projective identification excessively as opposed to a normal level of projective identification.

As Bion saw it, the challenge for the therapist, like the mother, was to "think" about the client's communication with the aim that the therapist would be able to link with the mind of the client and understand what could not be easily expressed in words. We can see from the above case study that the therapist worked hard to help Sam link with Bella's mind, and her other children too, that is, the therapist tried to help Sam to think about what her children might be thinking. Furthermore, the route into this was the process of the therapist herself thinking about the mind of Sam. Bion conceived of this process as a thinking dualism, the thinking mind of the therapist and the mind of the client working together. As Winnicott had claimed that there was "no such thing as a baby", that is, in the beginning there is always a baby and mother as one nursing couple, so Bion moved towards the idea that there was no such thing as a mind in isolation, or at least no such thing as a healthy mind in isolation. Bion advanced the theory of projective identification with the addendum that the task for mother therefore was to think about and contain, in her mind, the projections of the infant, transforming thoughts before presenting them back to the infant in a managed contained manner, thereupon forming a link.

Containing spaces and absent fathers

Bion (1959) noted especially where it was difficult to think about the communications from the client. He surmised that there were, what he called, attacks on thinking. Anyone who has heard the scream of an infant may attest to the blinding severance of any capacity to think. During the earliest stages of development the infant is a cauldron of needs where frustration, even minor frustrations such as an uncomfortable nappy, or a toy that cannot be grasped, can result in what seems to be unbearable tension. Bion (1959) clarified the facets of this parental challenge, that in the first place the involved the parent attempting to interpret situations, trying to find words or noises, either soothing or sharp, which reflect back the emotional states and situations that face the infant. Parenting becomes a continual process of experiential digestion, where transformation of emotionality is required in order to bring about increasing levels of emotional literacy in the child.

Bion (1959) described this concept of thinking and linking minds with a significant biological substrate. That the infant first took the mothers breast inside its mouth was the first link between what was felt inside and he developed a spatial model of the psyche which incorporated this mode of feeding, noting the repeating patterns of spatial relations, inside and outside experiences. Sucking and eating, then urinating and defecating were templates for a further psychic structuration based on the biological imperatives of inside and outside, and we saw these dynamics played out in the case study of Bella. Bion mapped these biological acts of inside and out, what is contained inside the body of the self and the body of mother, onto a psychological model, which became a theory of psychic containment. Bion deduced that the mind functioned in a way that was a biological derivative of the way in which food was digested in the alimentary canal. That is to say, the mind desired knowledge as the body desired food. Thus, when we talk about "chewing over someone's words" or words as "food for thought", we are hinting at a mental process which describes how we think.

Thus the terms "container" and "contained" came to denote this pattern of inside and outside relatedness (Bion, 1962). Thinking could be understood in this way, that is, the way in which the infant's accretions of the mind could be externalised and then contained in the mind of the mother. The mentation of emotions could be understood thereafter as a process of mental containment that was as essential to the infant wellbeing as the experience of bodily holding. Bion had indeed arrived at an articulation of the experience of holding in mind; it was a concept or realisation that was a "theoretical tour de force", according to Hinshelwood (1989, p. 189). Bion's model of "container–contained" offered a universal account of human nature where, in normal development, the ebb and flow of exchange between two persons (self and other) results in a child feeling contained and held in mind. It was an innovative theory of thinking that offered a new synthesis, perhaps even a cognitive theory of the emotions. The container–contained conception might be described as a schema which raises the concept of projective identification to a general theory of human functioning that could be applied to the relationship between people, groups, between thoughts, ideas, and experiences.

But as well as containment between people, we might also think about containing spaces. We do well generally to consider the architectural spaces of therapy, and there is a lack of outsight when it comes to what therapeutic spaces look like and how they shape minds. For instance, Daniel, age five, lost his tooth in the school therapy room in the morning. All the children who came after Daniel felt the impact of the lost tooth. Word had got round that Daniel's tooth had fallen out in his session and that it had been lost. The children later that morning and then in the afternoon were both unsettled and excited in equal measure at the prospect that they might happen across the missing tooth. Two children actively searched for it during their sessions.

Sometimes it seems necessary to be aware of what took place in the previous client's session, especially if it was a session that another therapist has conducted because it can feel like the room itself has a memory. A previous child might even leave a visible trace of their session, and sometimes it is more pronounced than a trace, as was the case with Daniel's tooth. Unspoken thoughts, split off feelings, a splatter of unnoticed paint, the empty space of a stolen toy, a trail of glitter, a secreted car in the sand tray, a fizz and a frazzle all give the room a memory. We might say the therapy room contains an emotional life; it holds the reverberations of feelings felt during sessions. The room harbours the unsaid. What happens, for example, for the child who jettisons part of their psyche in an act of projection and the therapist fails to receive it, like a crumpled picture in the bin? Might the communication be "collected" in the following session where the next "therapeutic couple" are differently attuned. Philosophers grapple with the notion; "If an acorn drops in a forest and no-one is there to hear it, does it make a sound?" In the case of the shared consulting room, an acorn dropped in one session may well become a tree in the next. Therapists need to embrace some of the more elastic possibilities of the dynamic mind and the containing therapeutic space.

Containment is both a space and a process that takes place within that space. There has been a growing interest in the intersubjective space or the "analytic third" (Ogden, 2004) of the therapeutic relationship. This is, essentially, the mental amalgam of both client and therapist. Aron (2006) uses a number of metaphors such as the idea of a seesaw, or strange attractors, or the compass, in order to convey how the intersubjectivity between client and therapist is a dynamic event. We might say that the consulting room itself becomes part of the therapeutic triangulation and operates as the primary container. It is not unusual for a distressed child to run to the therapy room in a school when the therapist is absent and find containment therein. Children have been known, on occasion, to barricade themselves within the room when the therapist has finished the session for it has become imbued with a meaning in and of itself.

Running a group for troubled boys between the ages of eight and nine years old, the therapist noted early on in the first session that the boys were exhibiting personas and caricatures of a particular construct of masculinity. There were karate chops, hard faces, swearing, and swagger. At one point one of the boys got up and moved over to another boy, squaring up to him. The therapist remarked; "Ah, I've misunderstood. I thought we were in a room at school, but we're in the middle of an Xbox game". After a rash of excited exchange the boys started to settle and a closer engagement emerged. The therapist's intervention in this case seemed to be rather elliptical, but the reference to an Xbox game seemed to contain the excess of male energy in the room. In other words the therapist was able to "think" about what might be felt in the group, and then able to put this into words. If the therapist's hunch was correct, the interpretation transformed the room from violent imaginative gaming space into containing classroom. The boys in the group wanted to know why they had been chosen for the group and after alighting upon what they thought was their "badness", they all concluded that their shared experience of not living with, or having a great deal of contact with their fathers, was their common ground. Their fathers were estranged from the boy's lives by prison, domestic violence, new families, or long working hours. They had intuited that this made them vulnerable to being put in the bin so to speak. In session three the boys were given play dough and invited to make a self-portrait. All but one of the six created long, cylindrical structures, two with bulbous heads, one with two spheres at the base. They waved them around and giggled. Draw your own conclusions, but the female therapist felt she needed to understand the centrality of the penis to these boys' identities. In amongst the maelstrom of feeling about their fathers' absence, indifference, aggression, in amongst their mother's stories of fear, abandonment, disappointment, and criticality they could be sure there was a penis of which they too were in possession. The play dough "willies" perhaps offered a symbolic peer sense of containment, in the absence of a father, the group identity with the presence of a thoughtful therapist, offered a new synthesis of a safe containing space.

Another young client, a ten-year-old boy, in one session referred to his father as a "sperm donor". The term felt borrowed from his mother, but the therapist wondered what it was like for the boy's father to be reduced to a seed. Another boy, Stuart, who had actually been conceived by donor insemination, knew nothing of his father other than he worked in a bank, and that he could contact him when he was eighteen if he wished. Stuart had significant difficulties transitioning between the classroom and the therapy room, likewise he could not move from classroom to playground, from numeracy to literacy, from laptop to book. Teaching assistants would have to "step stone" or "scaffold" him between spaces or engage in bargaining to manage these transitions. The therapist wondered if the nature of his preconception contributed to his "spatial mapping". He was unable to differentiate between male and female, was unconvinced by those in authority, and appeared to oscillate between being a babbling baby and wise sage from one moment to the next. The therapist wondered if Stuart's spatial struggles found any accord with the fact that the sperm used to conceive him did not go directly from penis to inside of mother, it took a pit stop in a laboratory to be cleaned and therefore it existed in a series of "transitional containers" before it arrived in the final container. It was as if A did not link to B, there did not seem to be a containing primary triangulation.

Although reverie and containment are maternal roles, it is perhaps the containment offered by father that serves to contain the mother, who in turn then is able to contain the child.

It is not unusual these days for young boys to be looking around for male role models in the absence of their own father. In the above vignettes the material points towards a missing paternal containment. Is it possible that there is a difference between maternal and paternal containment? We think there is. We might say there are two types of containment; (i) endoskeletal and (ii) exoskeletal, the former referring to the inside experience of mother's containment, the latter belonging to a more externally derived experience of paternal containment. The endoskeletal containment begins with the experience of being inside mother before moving to a marsupial sense of containment where there is a transition between inside and out. This inside-out experience of maternal containment is contrasted with the outside-in containment offered by father.

Elements of virtual containment

Some boys dealing with the pain and pang of paternal absence only see their fathers' in contact centres or on prison visits. In these spaces there is a different kind of physical containment, we might call it a "brick mother", to borrow Henri Rey's idea. Young boys in these situations imagine what they will grow up to be. They seek out versions of their adult selves spending more time in the company of virtual father figures than their actual ones. Damon, aged nine, reported that he had not spoken a word to anyone between leaving school the previous day and returning the following morning but had spent several hours playing computer games. Many young children are playing computer games well into time allocated for sleep with night, day, dream, reality, and virtuality blending into a sleepy, hazy hinterland. These virtual worlds are the new psychic retreats, offering a virtual techno-containment that may be dangerously autistic.

Some of these boys come to the attention of therapists who hear that they have been sitting alone in their rooms with their controllers, accompanied by disembodied voices issuing instructions or hit rates into their headsets, often in combat situations, with weapons in "their" hands. We might well wonder how this reshapes not only the relational field, but also mental space itself. There are some studies currently taking place using avatars in the treatment of people suffering from schizo-phrenia, but generally therapy rooms are "old school" in terms of the materials they provide for children to play with. Even so, therapists need to have "new school" sensibilities. It is not unusual for therapists to find themselves recreating virtual environments and narratives with physical resources that early pioneers of play therapy would have used, until children can settle into the real space of the therapy room with an actual other.

Therapists need to understand the virtual cultures within which children are wrapped. Disney's *Frozen* (2013) the highest grossing ani-mated film taking in over a billion dollars at the box office (BBC, 2014) seems to have its finger on the pulse. With lyrics such as "the past is in the past" and "the fears that once controlled me can't get to me any-more" and "let it go". In one primary school the therapist was privy to the heartfelt, whole school in the end of year six show singing along to "Let it go". The collective voice was poignant and elsewhere yearning considering the subject of moving on and the letting go of the fear of loss and loss itself. There was something containing about the children singing together. With a particularly disparate class the school thera-pist suggested to the teacher that they sing a song together each morn-ing. From Greek chorus to miner's choirs, from Hillsborough Requiem through to nursery lullabies passed down through the ages, the shared voice holds and contains the ruptures in our collective being.

Girls seem to find bonding from reciting lyrics in sync, lacing the language of mother tongue in shared voice. Words are containers of meaning, feeling, and ancestry and when combined with music they can journey us back to the orchestra of uterine life. The percussive beat of mother's heart, the whistling whine of tubular activity, the amniotic whoosh, the hum, gurgle, and gulp of digestive turbulence, the vari-able pitch of maternal voice filtered through a watery viscosity. Because whilst the foetus neither inhales nor swallows, as their digestive and respiratory systems lie inchoate in wait, and their eyes remain unsee-ing, they do hear. Therefore one of the first part object relations after placenta, umbilicus, and uterus is the mother's voice. When this process is prematurely interrupted, and baby needs to be contained in an incu-bator, it is worth considering how this early experience might shape the protomental psyche in a particular way (MacDonald, 2015).

Another element of virtual containment is the biological impact of pharmaceuticals, which seek to provide a level of psychic and behavioural control for conditions such as attention deficit hyperactivity disorder (ADHD). The medication interrupts neural pathways carrying internal communication, and this interruption also alters the process of external communication. Trying to work therapeutically with these children can be a challenge. A therapist was working with a very lively, engaging child when he was medicated part way through treatment. When she next saw him after the holidays, he seemed considerably altered. She felt unable to reach him and found herself picking up an empty kitchen towel roll and looking for him through it. He came to the other end and they met eye to eye. "Ah, there you are. I thought I'd lost you," the therapist said. They sat and talked for a few minutes and then the child "drifted away" once more. The therapist felt inconsolable. She felt that child looked at her with what she described as a "void communication". She couldn't think, but recalled the words of the renowned sculptor Anthony Caro who said of his work that it had "an inside but no centre" (from the blurb from his exhibition at the Yorkshire Sculpture Park, 2015).

On another occasion, a therapist was standing in front of a board outside the classroom of her client who had recently been subject to a change in his medication for his ADHD. He wanted to show her his self-portrait in amongst his classmates. But when they looked and looked they couldn't find it for a good few minutes. The therapist felt anxious that the portrait might have gone missing, until at last they spotted it. The child said, "We were looking right at me but couldn't see me." The words seemed to sum up what it can be like to be in a room with a heavily medicated child.

Reflections on containment

To summarise, the premise of containment is that the client brings an array of overwhelming feelings that they cannot bear or hold onto themselves. The therapist's challenge is one of offering an ordinary mind to digest the client's projections offering good food for thought, gauging how the client manages to digest this food for thought, and thereafter noting when the client repudiates or attacks the food for thought. The intuitive therapist is attuned to the client's wavelength and is able to identify, receive, and hold onto that which the client brings to therapy. The state of mind of the client may be represented in what they say, how they look, or in their play activity in the session. The exchange may be characterised by the client having strong feelings, perhaps feeling angry or let down or neglected. The therapist's response is to receive these communications and experience them. Bion tells us that the therapist must suffer too, that is the burden of reflexivity, and this suffering is more indicative than sympathy and more searching than empathy. Bion argues that if the therapist is not suffering, then they are not doing their job properly. So rather than ignoring or shelving what the client brings to therapy, the therapist strives to think about what the client feels, and drawing on their own experiences to feel somewhere what the client might be feeling. Projective identification in this sense can be said to require the hooks inside the therapist; if containment is the product of projective identification it happens via the experiential hooks within the therapist.

The therapeutic transformation for the client is the valuable discovery that something that seemed unbearable can, in actual fact, be thought about and survived. The therapist holds onto the feelings that the client has projected into them, contains them, and without being over-whelmed by them, communicates the experience back to the client in a way that the client can understand and manage. The aim in the long run is to help a client contain their own feelings. As to whether all pro-jections that the therapist has received need to be returned is subject to some debate, and sometimes it might well be the case that the material that the client has brought to therapy need not be returned. That is to say, if it is toxic then the therapist may discharge it in the same way that toxic biological waste is expunged. The therapist may feel exhausted at the end of a session and may need to deposit what the client has brought, either by making notes about the session and filing them away until next time, or by talking over issues in supervision. Sometimes the residual effect of a session may go on afterwards and therapists might find that some client's are; "playing on their mind", it might well be that the client has gone beyond being contained and it might feel like the client is trapped. In more extreme cases therapists can end up having disturbing dreams about clients (Winship, 1995) in a way that can feel like "unconscious bruising".

It is helpful to consider the concept of containment in terms of the space of the therapy. It is possible to talk about a containing milieu or a containing environment, which amounts to the sum total of the variety of structures and relationships that impact on the child in the school. These interleaving structures may be routines, they may be set therapeutic sessions, they may even be rules, and taken together foster a containing milieu. We should also think about an architecture of containment that includes a creative therapeutic space that can be easily subject to temperature and light control and resourced with plenty of materials for creative play. Many therapists are at pains to maintain the room as found, clearing any trace of a previous inhabitant, fostering a kingdom of isolation when actually therapist and client should be working toward the reality of the populated maternal lap and the tolerance of sharing space and resources. Containment may be increased by emphasising the space as analytic third.

Containment has been proven to be an indispensable idea that has been applied with increasing frequency in supervision and in accounts of case practice. We might say that the idea has proliferated because it has been a concept that works and therefore creates its own good press. The idea barely needs to be introduced to trainees, clients, and supervisees, before it starts to assume value as it is re-tested by each new generation of practitioners. There is a process of concept hypothecation (early stage), application and triangulation (middle stage), and then dissemination (final stage), from which a good idea becomes embedded. Subject to further testing, the concept becomes familiar and successful out of a quiet cycle of subjective case study research. To some extent this is the way in which sound knowledge assimilation has worked in psychotherapy discourses for well over a century now. Clinician researchers in psychotherapy rarely make grand claims to any particular scientific truths, instead case study findings that purport to be partial truths. The proviso is that over time universal schemas avail themselves to become accumulative viable truths. Containment is one such truth to come of age we might say.

CHAPTER FIVE

On curiosity—transference and interpretation

Brief

We make a case here for therapists to be more inquisitive about what is happening with their clients. Too often therapists tread too softly, as if somehow to speak openly is out of turn. But many of the children and young people who come to therapy have lost the capacity to speak openly. The self is a distant shore. It is not always viable to believe that each child has a natural sense of who they are, because many young children who come to therapy have had lives that have been out of kilter with what we would hope is the ordinary yield of human nature. For some children nature has not been fair. The presence of therapist needs to be purposeful and audible.

The skill of asking open-ended questions has been a technique in counselling and psychotherapy that dates back to the 1970s and is probably mostly associated with the pioneering work of Gerald Egan. An open-ended question frames the exchange with the client in such a way that the client cannot respond to the therapist with a simple; "yes" or "no" (which would be the effect of a closed question), instead the client is invited to proffer a more elaborate articulation. An example of open question would be; "how are you feeling?", whereas a closed question might be; "do you feel sad?" Although the technique of open-ended questioning might seem a bit like tricking the client into speaking openly, it is nonetheless an excellent conversational tool, which can open up a dialogue in therapy.

The idea of asking questions has, however, more lately been subject to criticism in some schools of therapy thought. That is to say, asking questions is frowned upon because somehow a question is seen as the therapist directing or leading the client. For example Geldard and Geldard (2012) assert that the counsellor should not ask too many questions, indeed they say it is; "dangerous to ask too many questions" (Geldard & Geldard, 2012, p. 14). Actually, in reality, the danger lies in the fact that therapists often ask too few questions. It is unhelpful to cast the counsellor and psychotherapist as a passive listening agent. Especially with younger clients the therapist needs to be more active. We think it is worth rescuing the idea that questions are generally a good thing in therapy and we want to frame this in terms of a new idea which we are calling "therapeutic curiosity". Therapeutic curiosity is an ingredient of a culture of enquiry which includes; therapist self-scrutiny, being inquisitive about the client, and not taking small detail for granted. Curiosity is a deconstructive approach that seeks to identify how the client ticks. The idea of a culture of enquiry might be applied to a whole milieu or treatment community, and we might think of the classroom operating within a framework of a culture of enquiry. The client-therapist relationship is likewise sewn together in a micro culture of enquiry.

Curiosity should not be a one-way street, and the aim is for curiosity to become a co-constructed process between the client and the therapist, with the aspiration that one day the client will indeed become their own therapist. But in the first place the psychotherapist needs to create a milieu where curiosity is stirred. Painful experiences of being scrutinised or put upon, or past experiences of abuse or neglect may have led to a thwarted curiosity. Indeed, the client might find the thoughtful curiosity of the therapist as difficult to manage. So the therapist may need to take a lead in helping the client become curious. This will necessarily involve the therapist asking questions somewhere along the line.

In this chapter we map out a framework for what we call "structured curiosity" which builds on a theory of transference and the technique of interpretation. The technique of interpretation has also often been misunderstood. Across the broader family of psychotherapies we have heard counselling and psychotherapy trainees saying that they; "don't do interpretation", and even many psychoanalytic therapists seem to interpret as a last resort. We think this is a worrying state of closed mindedness that dents curiosity, so it is timely to reframe interpretation and seek to vitalise the notion of interpretation as communication that expresses curiosity. We also develop the idea of different levels of interpretation moving from explanatory to descriptive and through to more intensified depths of curiosity (Alvarez, 2010). We frame these interpretive frames as a model of "convexive" and "inflective" interpretation. With the added dimension of understanding transference, we argue that "structured curiosity" is a new essential ingredient of a therapist's repertoire of skills and knowledge.

The playground of transference

Erikson (1950, 1968) proposed predictable changes in personality over the lifespan based on eight psychosocial stages of development. It is notable that Erikson posited that each stage of transition was precipitated by some sort of crisis. Erikson referred to these as threshold points in maturation where upward progress is accompanied by the need to overcome some conflict. The idea of making a link between crisis and maturation is useful for therapists who encounter clients who have either not passed through some stages of crisis, or have got stuck at some point. Erikson steers us to engage with the ructions and abruptions of psychic change and each of these stages of crisis bring with them a number of interpersonal conflicts, to a greater or lesser extent with peers and siblings, but often with authority figures such as parents, teachers, and also therapists.

Conflict focused approaches to therapy, after Erikson, therefore embrace the necessity of working through conflict as a key ingredient of therapy. The difference between conflict focused therapy and solution focused approaches might be one of the ways we can track the emergence of different paradigms in the field of mental health in the late twentieth century. Exploratory based approaches that have been centred on the relational and experiential antecedents to development, including trauma, and these have been founded on a different set of premises to therapies which have emerged from more positivist philosophies. Positivist and solution focused strategies seek out tactics and routes that might lead to progress, for an example cognitive behavioural therapy (CBT), meanwhile the demeanour of the conflict focused therapist is characterised by an aplomb that steels itself for the battle ahead. While the solution focused therapist can be upbeat about the behavioural possibilities of change, the conflict focused therapist is braced for the interpersonal antagonism which might be the source of working through the prior psychic unease as it unfolds in the here-and-now.

We would say that transference and countertransference fall into the category of therapy as a process of conflict resolution, especially where the transference is a negative one and indicates where development has got stuck. That is to say, clients bring to therapy the shadows of their experiences from elsewhere and so it is here that the therapist encounters the client, in light of prior experiences. Regardless of a denominated school of approach, to have at least some rudimentary theoretical grasp of transference, if only as a safety precaution, is sensible. That is to say, if we know a client has been aggressive to females in the past, then it is worth knowing this before another female therapist is allocated to work with a client.

Yet there are some practitioners who regard transference as an unruly intrusion in the client-therapist relationship. For example Geldard and Geldard (2012) talk about therapists who; "suspect that transference is occurring ..." (p. 125), suggesting that transference is an occasional matter that needs to be treated with suspicion. This view of transference would seem to miss the crucial point that transference is a universal facet of human nature that shapes all interpersonal relationships. Patterns of attachment and relating are replayed throughout our lives, not just in therapy, so a theory of transference helps us understand how a young client will relate to their therapist, but also how they will relate to their teacher, their peers and so on.

Freud recognised from the outset the emergence of strong feelings on the part of the client towards the therapist and that these feelings in the present were drawn from previous relationships. At first glance, he thought that the remnants of past experience, as they became manifest in the session, might be an obstacle to the work of building a therapeutic alliance. However as time went by, he recognised that transference was central to the process of understanding and unravelling the patient's difficulties and he began advocating working with the transference rather than trying to edit it out. In 1910 Freud made reference to another phenomenon which he called countertransference;

> We have become aware of the counter-transference, which arises in
> the analyst as a result of the patient's influence on his unconscious
> feelings, and we are almost inclined to insist that he shall recog-
> nise this counter transference in himself and overcome it. (Freud,
> 1910, p. 144).

Initially countertransference feelings were regarded as hazardous, as if by having a countertransference reaction the analyst was losing their capacity for objectivity. However, later colleagues began to notice that countertransference reactions often provided helpful insight into the emotional exchange between therapist and client, in other words, the client's past experiences could be alive in the here-and-now insofar as the therapist might end up feeling as if indeed they were behaving like someone from the client's past. Paula Heimann (1950) especially promulgated the idea that the cool detachment cultivated by many psychoanalysts was liable to render their work, and interpretations, sterile; "... the analyst's response to his patient within the analytic situation represents one of the most important tools for his work. The counter transference is an instrument of research into the patient's unconscious" (Heimann, 1950, p. 74). For example, a therapist was working with a six-year-old girl who said she wanted to; "scoop out her mother's face". The therapist had struggled to make sense of what this meant, but had some hunch that this communication was important, and might help her understand why the client had been diagnosed along the autistic spectrum. In a session a few days later the therapist met the gaze of the client, but had a rather unnerving sense that the client could not actually see her face, and that rather than looking into her eyes, she felt the client was disappearing into the dark space of the pupils. The therapist indeed felt as if she had no face, and she wondered if this was a countertransference, that is, she felt like what it might be to be the young client's mother.

Structured curiosity

So it is our assertion that structured curiosity begins with the therapist being alert to the transference and countertransference. But what do we mean by curiosity? Worst case scenarios are sometimes the place where we can see the clearest need for practice development. We conducted an audit of twenty special case reviews of completed suicides among school age children and we noted that there were several cases where school counsellors had been involved in working with the young people prior to the suicide. We wonder if there is more that could have been done. Seung-Hui Cho, who killed thirty-two people in 2007 at Virginia Tech in the United States, had been to see the University counsellor. There have been other cases in the US and the UK where there has been devastating violence at a school. When we reflect on these cases, including occasions from our first-hand experience of working with older clients who have taken their own lives, we are prompted to wonder if something more might have been done.

Counselling and psychotherapy can be too passive. Therapists of course need to listen first and foremost, but being a sounding board is not enough. This is especially the case with younger clients. Being alongside the client is necessary, but the therapist needs to have the capacity to link with the mind of their young client. More recently the idea of "mentalization" has become a useful theory and descriptor for the challenge of working the space between minds. Mentalization points us in the direction of a therapeutic encounter where the client has the experience of what it is like to have someone "thinking" about you (Allen, Fonagy, & Bateman, 2008). Mentalization can be thought of as both a process and a situation whereby the client comes to experience a "mind within a mind", that is to say, the client develops a sense that the therapist's mind is alive within their own. Within the orbit of the concept of a mind within a mind, curiosity is a vital ingredient in the process of helping the client's mind come alive.

The client might have a fragile unformed sense of what it is like to be held in mind by someone else. The neglect of thought might be physically apparent for instance when the client is emaciated or undernourished, or has ill-fitting unwashed clothes. The neglect might be borne from the mind of a parent or carer too preoccupied with other concerns, too absent, remote or perhaps unwell. The experience of being "thought about" by a therapist can offer a new beginning, a fresh synthesis of what it is to be thought about. But the experience of having an interested therapist, at least at first, might also be unsettling for the client. Lucy, eight years old, was referred for counselling because she was prone to being disruptive in class. At playtime she was overbearing with playmates, but her bullying manner seemed to belie the part of her that felt invisible at home where she was submerged by elder siblings and out of the mind of her mother who was otherwise struggling on her own to keep herself together. Lucy's imposition on her peers seemed to be a compensatory attempt to make her-self present in a world where, at her core, she felt absent. In the session, alone with her therapist for the first time Lucy was uncomfortable and suspicious of her therapist's attention; "you're trying to read my mind", said Lucy recoiling from her therapist's gaze. The therapist, who was herself a relatively new trainee replied; "no, I'm not", trying to put

Lucy at ease. It was a missed opportunity for the therapist, because she was indeed interested in ascertaining what was going on in Lucy's mind. The defensive response, feigning disinterest, might well have served to confirm Lucy's alienation and her belief that people might not really be interested in what she was thinking.

In actual fact it is not uncommon for clients to "accuse" therapists of trying to read their minds. And the response commonly is defensive. Curiosity can be a risk and thinking into the mind of the client can require some mental tenacity. Young clients try and block out the mind of the therapist; we see it in children suffering from autism that they try and avoid eye contact, as if by avoiding the gaze of the therapist they can protect themselves from any emotional contact. Furthermore, it is perhaps understandable that therapists also want to avoid inhabiting the mind of the client, albeit unconsciously, even for a short while. The interior of the young client's mind might be brim full with hurt and sadness, and therapists can too easily sit passively alongside a client without ever feeling what it is like to be inside the mind of the client. Indeed, there are some clinical approaches, such as behaviour therapy, which set out a series of practice axioms that intercept intimacy and ensure that the therapist is only ever superficially engaged with the client, focusing on actions and behaviours as opposed to thoughts and feelings. The behaviour therapist will set behavioural tasks for the client, for example touching door handles and so on, thus the therapist-client relationship is relegated to an encounter at some distance.

But it is not just behaviour therapists who procedurally defend against what is hurting in the mind of the client. Avoiding questions or by not offering opinions for fear of being seen as directive, keeps the space between client and therapist at a distance. This remote approach is presented as the demeanour of a non-directive approach, but the effect is a lack of genuine intimacy with the client. Without being intimately *au fait* with what is on the client's mind, through the process of being curious, it is not possible to know what troubles the client. Bion (1970) argues that it is otherwise a duty and an obligation for the therapist to think about and "suffer" with the client (p. 19). Without that suffering, the therapist cannot know the client. Therapist curiosity might come with a health warning if, as Bion argues, it entails an element of suffering with the client. That is to say, if the therapist finds out more about the client's mind, then there will be a consequence of contact with the hurt that the client brings to therapy. Most therapists are probably naturally curious and sometimes it is training that can take away that natural curiosity. When practitioners can hold onto their curiosity, especially when it is honed by technique and experience, the outcome can be most beneficial.

But curiosity is hard won. Therapists might sometimes feel that they are stuck to the same spot, spending session after session with the client repeating patterns of activity which suggest that the client is no more engaged this week than last. Therapy can often be more mundane than it is profane, so keeping curiosity alert and alive is a challenge to the imagination and spirit of the therapist. But where there is curiosity, there is always hope. But here's the rub, how is it that curiosity can be trained and sustained? And if we can train and sustain it, how do we go about honing and even researching it?

Structured curiosity—assessment of the family at home

If we are to know the nature of the transference then it is necessary to get a picture of the family. Freud referred to the "family under the couch", that is to say, the client does not come alone to therapy, rather there are many presences occupying the space in the therapy room. Sometimes the therapy room can seem quite crowded with parents, siblings, friends, teachers, and others, it is not so much that the family is under the couch, rather they are all over the place, in the doll's house, in the sand-tray and so on. We do well to borrow the family therapy idea of the "identified client", that is to say, we think of the client in therapy who is there by dint of representing a wider network of difficulties in a whole family system. It is often the case that it is family members, both past and present, who are the ones who really need the therapy but, by force of circumstances, have not been able to get therapy. Previous generations might well have seeded the faulty coping strategies or embedded unhelpful relationship patterns which have been then imprinted on the client, who at last brings them to the attention of someone trained to understand how families work and don't work.

So it is necessary to build up a picture of the client's family background, including people beyond the family who might feature in the constellation of the client's network. There are two simple ways of swiftly drawing up a picture of the clients network of relationships: first, with a family tree (see Figure 1) and second, within a family constellation map

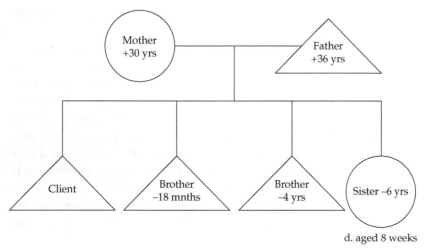

Figure 1. Family tree example.

(Figure 2). A basic family tree mapping tool can serve as a visual mind-map for the therapist and this source family tree can be embellished with notes over time, eventually providing a picture of the client's network of relationships as they come in and out of focus across time. Where possible, with older clients, it can be a useful exercise for the

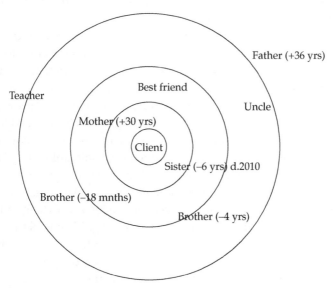

Figure 2.

family tree or constellation map to be drawn up during the session with the client being guided by the therapist.

In the examples of a family tree (see Figure 1) we can see that the client has two male siblings, and a deceased sister. The family tree takes the root age from the client, using shapes to denote gender. It is possible to see family characteristics such as age of parents at birth, and then any significant losses, such as the loss of a sibling, or a miscarriage, and so on. The family tree map can be extended to include grandparents, and in the case of blended families, the family tree of half-siblings and step siblings. In the case of blended families, the family tree can be a complex diagram, but also an illuminating one. The family tree diagram always takes the root age from the client, using shapes to denote gender, and lines to show connections, and broken lines to denote divorce and separations.

In the constellation map (Figure 2), the visual map works outwards with the client placed at the centre of the map. The client is asked to plot significant relationships, placing the people who are felt to be closest proximal to the centre of the map.

The family constellation map, or eco-map as it has been called (Hartman, 1995), provides a visual diagram of the key relationship in the clients life. We can see in the eco-map example (Figure 2) that the client's father is a rather distant figure who is felt by the client to be no more significant than the teacher.

Where the family is more complicated we can use lines to denote relationships; for example broken line might be a code to point to a relationship that is remote or jagged lines to denote relationships that are characterised by conflict, often with close relations. Strong lines might be used to show where relationships are solid. One might well see a strong line between the client and a rather remote figure such as a head teacher who the client has described in ways which suggest a strong secure attachment. Where the client has step-relations, half-siblings and so on, the therapist and client will need to take the time to develop what might end up as a complex family tree and constellation. The family tree and constellation map can be built up over time to include extended family members including grandparents and other significant relationships. These family tree maps can be a useful shared reference source for the therapist and the client. The pressure is eased on the therapist trying to remember the names and places of the client's system, and in turn the client can see clearly the structure of their network of relationships, which they can edit. In time we might expect to see some technology advances which would allow the therapist (and client) to build up these maps using computer software that would allow for some more sophisticated coding of relationships.

By clarifying who it is that the client brings to therapy with them, the therapist is able to cut through the melee of the presence of others in the session in order to establish some immediacy of contact with the client themselves.

Interpretation

Close observation to detail is a commendable facet of curiosity. The good-enough therapist finds herself prompted by her observations during play activities and compelled to ask herself questions like; why is this child burying his dad in the sand? Why does this child always go to the toilet mid-session even though he has had a break just before I picked him up? Why did this child choose to paint in red today? Why does this child stand in that same spot every week before embarking on any activity? Why do I feel so derelict at the end of every session, even though the client leaves the room skipping? After a while of working with the client, the therapist might begin to speculate about the answers to some of these questions. It might well be the case that the buried dad is indicative of the child dealing with the loss of a father who is away in prison, or the therapist might know that the child has been in a fight in the playground, and so is painting in red because they feel bloodied or angry. If the therapist begins to ask questions about what might be happening for the client, we can call this a hypothetical interpretation. An interpretation is first and foremost an educated guess that takes the form of a question. It is a thought, in the mind of the therapist, that attempts to put two elements together; first, the data from the client in terms of activity or words, and then second, what it is that the therapist already knows about the client.

The therapist initially forms and holds in their mind a hypothesis based on a combination of data that has been gathered either from observation or from knowledge accrued about the client's history which might have come from the client or from a significant other (parent, teacher). The therapist might have intuition about what is happening, for example; the child is burying the father and replaying this because they are struggling with feeling sad. It may be enough for the therapist to keep this interpretation in mind, to wait and discover if the interpretation is correct without ever voicing the interpretation. For instance, in one session Daniel, aged nine, was busily splashing brown paint all over his page without much attempt at making his painting into anything recognisable. Daniel had been struggling since his father had gone to prison, so the therapist at first thought this was progress for Daniel to splash paint around as he was usually reticent to play freely. But shortly afterwords the therapist began to have a hunch that Daniel was angry. Daniel's paint splashing appeared to be escalating, and so the therapist thought she might make need to see if she could offer Daniel some sense of containment by naming or interpreting what he was feeling. But just as the therapist was about to verbalise her interpretation as a question; which would have been something like; "Daniel I wonder if you are angry today?" Daniel put down his paintbrush, folded his arms and said grumpily; "I'm cross".

Verbalising an interpretation is a question of timing. In Daniel's case the interpretation remained a thought in the therapist's mind, and in the end Daniel was able to find the words to express how he was feeling. Therapists are too often reluctant to make the most of their curiosity, as if there is an embargo on their natural communicative curiosity. In another session the therapist asked Daniel; "I wonder if you buried your daddy in the sand because you miss him?" The question was a communicative event that conveyed the therapist's curiosity and concern at the same time, as well as putting into words what Daniel might have been struggling to articulate. We are naturally curious creatures, and children especially so. Daniel said he wasn't missing his Dad, and the therapist surmised that Daniel was relieved that his father was in prison, that the absence of his father had offered some respite from a domestic situation that was fraught with violence. Winnicott reassures us that it is okay for therapists to get something wrong, that this is the real world where we live. We would concur that it is better to wonder and get it wrong than to leave the child cut off adrift and alone, that it is best to try and convey curiosity about what is happening than to sit on in silence. If the interpretation hypothesis is wrong, at least the client can orientate the therapist to what is true. If an interpretation is done with the best of intentions, it conveys the essential ingredient of curiosity and this will be affirming for the client; "my therapist knows me", or "my therapist wants to know me".

Interpretation offers something more substantial in an exchange than simply asking the client; "what are you doing?". An interpretation has the added dimension of speculation that is food for thought based on the therapist's knowledge of the client. Good supervisors will challenge supervisees about their reluctance to ask interpretative questions. When a child repeatedly gets a toy figure of Batman and makes him jump from heights such as shelves or drawers, and he does this in several consecutive sessions across several weeks, there are choices about reading this pattern of play. The therapist might say that the child just happens to like Batman and leave it at that. Indeed, many therapists are inclined to enquire no further. But clients should expect more of their therapist. When we "notice" that the child is mixed race and we notice that Batman is a white man covered in a black skin, we have something more to think about. When we "notice" that the client no longer lives with his father and things are difficult at home because the siblings are fighting, and then we know that Batman is a superhero who is called upon to govern the lawless, now, we are starting to get somewhere. To ask; "who is the Batman?", is a good question and if the therapist has some answer to this question, albeit speculatively, then it is good practice to pass on the knowledge to the client. The thought belongs to the client, even if the therapist thinks it. A failure to return this thought to the thinker might well be theft.

If we make informed guesses then the child will be encouraged to be curious too. The therapist's curious mind becomes the spur for an exchange of ideas. Providing the therapist is of sound enough mind, and has had enough therapy, then the therapist's mind that can act as a receptacle that can be the creative cradle of co-constructing knowledge. Freud's (1900) original concept of "interpretation" was always intended as a way of opening up conversation and it has so often been misunderstood. It is not uncommon for some people to refer to interpretation as the therapist "putting words into the client's mouth", or "inserting ideas". The concept of an authoritative interpretation was never Freud's intention. In the *Interpretation of Dreams* Freud (1900) tells us that the analyst's response to the dream should not impinge upon the dreamer's intelligence. In other words, the dreamer's own interpretation is always the first port of call. The therapist's first question is to ask the client what they make of the dream. Perhaps one of the misunderstandings of Freud's concept is the problem of the translation of the German word "deutung", which might well have been translated as "clarification" rather than "interpretation". The concept of clarification summons up an altogether different notion. Clarification suggests something that is more like a question, whereby the therapist begins by asking something that is speculative rather than definitive, for example, the delivery of a response to an element of case material might predicated by; "I wonder if your dream might indicate this ...?".

Doubt and curiosity are essential elements of interpretation. If one knows how to read Freud one can see throughout that he is so often notional with his understandings. He was self-critical almost to a fault, and in his writings he continually berates his own shortcomings, his inadequacy of theory, arguing that his ideas are merely preliminary foundations for others to deconstruct and then build upon. What we see in his method of interpretation, beginning with the "dream of Irma", is how each section of the dream and each fragment of information can be unpicked. He urged that nothing in the dream should be ignored, that each detailed point might have important meaning. Interpretation was his tool of curiosity, and his approach was detective-like. And he (Freud, 1901, 1905) later considered that meaning could be found behind other activities such as jokes, or slips of the tongue, Freudian slips so to speak. Interpretation was a tool for debate, for constructing the knowledge and understanding, and Freud was under no illusion that the process of construction was ultimately subject to the client's intelligence, with the therapist as a sort of servant of the truth;

> We do not pretend that an individual construction is anything more than a conjecture which awaits examination, confirmation and rejection ... In short we conduct ourselves on the model of familiar figure in one of Nestroy's farces—the manservant who has a single answer on his lips to every question or objection; "it will all become clear in the fullness of time". (Freud, 1937, p. 265)

The use of interpretation and the search for meaning proliferated among Freud's colleagues. And with the advent of play therapy techniques with children the idea of interpretation was taken to a new explanatory level.

Convexive and inflective interpretations

When Strachey (1933) considered the Freudian behest of interpretation, he argued that there had been no precise definition of its nature. Rather, interpretation had been invested with the qualities of something of; "a magic weapon" (1933, p. 141). The vicissitudes of opinion about the use of interpretation were so varied among his colleagues, some thought that to interpret too rashly or too soon would run the risk of scaring the client away, whereas other colleagues felt that a failure to interpret soon enough would risk losing the client because the client would feel that there was not enough to hold on to. The binary of "too much too soon" versus "too little too late" perhaps characterises the on-going debate about interpretation. Some analysts urged caution in making interpretation in case there were errors of judgement, while others argued that it was necessary to test interpretations when in doubt, in order to clarify meaning and intent. Strachey's attempt to develop a classification system was designed to bring some structure to the debate. Strachey adopted the term "mutative interpretation" to describe an interpretation which brought about a change in the patient's perception. He said there were two phases to interpretation; firstly interpretations which were "immediate", designed to impact upon id impulses, and second those which were said to be "deep" with the target of changing super-ego functioning. Both types of interpretation Strachey said were intended to reach the patient's id impulses, but a deep interpretation was aimed at changing super-ego functioning.

Klein's approach to interpretation was more fluid than Strachey's structural approach, and she seemed more on the side of "when in doubt, interpret" using the technique with gusto (Segal, 1986). Indeed, as a result of her work analysing young children, Klein developed an approach to play therapy whereby she would deploy interpretation in order to provide something of a running commentary to the silent drama in the play activities of her young clients. Her approach became known as the "interpretive technique" (Klein, 1932) as she spotted the parallels in the way in which children would use play materials to create scenarios drama that resembled the drama of dreams which Freud (1900) had shown to be the "Royal Road to the Unconscious". Klein also noted the way in which children would move between sequences of play in a way that was not dissimilar to the way in which adult analytic would "free associate" with words and ideas. And so, she thought it feasible to apply the technique of interpretation as a means to discovering the unconscious meanings in the dreamlike, free associative play of children. Thus came into being the "interpretive technique".

Klein dispensed with the conventions of putting clients at ease, at least ostensibly on the surface, and instead the interpretative technique attempted to establish direct contact with the child's unconscious.

Hannah Segal (1986) provided a compelling account of the way in which the interpretive technique could quickly bring about transformations. In her example she recounted a child of two and three quarters years old who had been referred to her because she was afraid of the dark and suffering from nightmares. Segal tells us that when she met the child for the first time, the child was anxious and unwilling to come into the consulting room. So what did Segal do? Did she offer reassurance and tell the young client that it would be alright to go into the room because there were nice toys to place with? Or did she tell the child that everything would alright and that Mummy would be just outside? No, she did neither. Instead she offered an interpretation; "You are afraid because you do not know me". She cut to the unconscious chase, so to speak, and spoke out loud the young client's anxieties. The interpretation seemed to do the trick because the child then entered the room. Once in the consulting room the child began to hesitantly explore the room and the toys and Segal tells us that she interpreted; "you are afraid of the unknown, like you are afraid of the dark at night, but you are also curious about what goes on in the dark". Within a few weeks, the child is no longer hesitant and is willingly coming into session.

A less experienced therapist might try to be reassuring with an anxious young client, perhaps by telling them that there are nice things in the room, reassuring them and so forth. A less experienced therapist might try to put on a smile and sound friendly. Instead, Klein and Segal say put aside such conventions and niceties and address the unconscious conflict. So often reassurance can be empty rhetoric, but in the above example Segal's interpretation is appealing and reassuring because it is filled with knowledge about what is distressing. Using Strachey's classification, one might say that the first interpretation about the client being afraid of the therapist is an "immediate interpretation", while the second interpretation points away towards the conflict that is elsewhere (the dark night at home).

These two different elements of interpretation, that is, on the one hand an interpretation that is aimed at the immediacy of the therapeutic alliance in the "here-and-now", and on the other an interpretation that is focused on previous conflict which we think of as "then and there", might form the basis of a structure for interpretative curiosity. The first of these we might call an "inflective interpretation" that draws attention to the client-therapist relationship, and the second "then and there" interpretation as "convexive" (sic). This delineation is summarised in a diagram below.

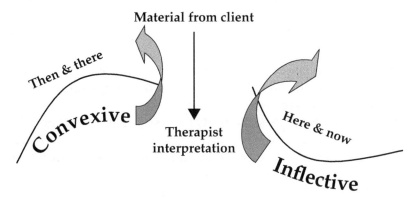

Figure 3. Diagram summarising convexive & inflective interpretations.

We can think of these different types of interpretation as mirrors that attempt to reflect back to the client elements of their experience. The idea of a mirroring process is meaningful here insofar as a convex mirror, which is out-turned, amplifies visual information, whereas an inflective mirror is turned inwards. A convexive interpretation that focuses attention on the client's past might be more akin to the sort of deep interpretation that Strachey describes as it seeks to root out elements of past conflict, which continues to exert strong influence on the client's present. We would say it is helpful for the therapist to keep track of the different types of interpretation that therapists are using during the passage of time in therapy. It might well be the case the it is more common-place for interpretations to be more inflective during the early part of therapy, that is to say, interpretations that draw attention to the immediacy of contact between therapist and client, before later starting to explore elements of prior experience. We might speculate that this is a necessary part of building of a therapeutic alliance between the client and the therapist whereby both become aware of the transference situation.

Of course the question of when to make an interpretation is important, and it is often down to the therapist's hunch or intuition, about when to speak and when to wait. Intuition is the key that is turned by curiosity. How much intuition is developed in psychotherapy training is not straightforward. The paradox of intuition—that is to say the word which breaks into; "in tuition"—is that it probably cannot be taught. Are people born with the intuitive capacity to be a good therapist? In all probability, there is something embedded in the therapist's imaginative and mental constitution that is the engine room of intuition which exists long before training begins. Training might well hone intuition. Perhaps the most important question is to think about what might inhibit intuition in practitioners. As a human potential we might say intuition can inhibited by anxiety, stress, or when a practitioner is preoccupied in times of personal adversity.

The clinical capacity to subjectively harness a "gut feeling" in order to arrive at a clinical judgement may be an anathema to practitioners who pursue objectivity in decision-making. It is not the case that there should be less intuition in clinical practice, rather it is the case that we should dedicate more time and research and ensure practitioners intuitive faculties are honed, primed, and maintained. A utopian vision of mental health services in some people's minds—some twenty, fifty or a hundred years hence—might have automatons and computers working with exact diagnostics capabilities, where heroic gene or biological modifications are researched to the hilt. It is unlikely. The advances in terms of the brain are much less substantial than what we have come to understand of the mind. Imagine a workforce of practitioners intuitively brilliant who have the capacity, in a moment or two, to read psychotic and depressed minds, and the ability to respond to clients with a deep emotional reflexivity, attuned and empathic.

Our intuitive capacities are harvested from outside-in experience, rather than something summoned up from within. Of course self-reflection is an essential facet of intuition, but one has to be wary of it appearing that there is too much time given over to self-reflection. One student trainee had the brazen title: "Myself, My Journey to Me". The triplicate reference to the self-conveyed something of the problem of the way in which counselling may seem to appear too therapist centred and not enough focus on the client. In cognitive behaviour therapy there is little in the way of personal reflection on how the therapist feels, rather training and supervision concentrates on techniques and tactics and what is happening to the client. CBT in this sense does seem to be laudably client-centred.

Final reflections

Interpretation is not the end point of any stage of process in therapy, rather it is intended to open up a conversation where the therapist and client can be curious about thoughts and feelings. If curiosity is a river that flows towards truth and knowledge, then interpretation is the source. Rather than offering summations of truth, interpretations begin tentatively as modified questions that aim to open up communication channels for discussion, exploration, and finally explanation. The challenge for the therapist is to maintain a sense of curiosity and willing open-mindedness long after the inquisitive shine of getting to know a client has long diminished. Indeed, the challenge is to remain curious across not just across one case, but across a career. Esteemed therapists, like Winnicott and Klein, research and revise their ideas long into their third age. A curious mind, we might say, is best borne from the wisdom that is the gift of age, but curiosity will also keep you young at heart. Age will not whither a curious mind.

CHAPTER SIX

On protecting—therapy as safeguarding

Brief

Play is the language of primary school counselling and psychotherapy. When seven-year-old Troy was running around the therapy room frantically tidying up and hiding the baby doll, it was not difficult for the therapist and supervisor to surmise that it was likely that the recent Social Care intervention, which culminated in the removal of one of his siblings, was being played out in the therapy room. Of course, play in therapy does not always equate with a recreation of experience elsewhere, for instance when children play with puppets where there are repeated fights, it does not necessarily mean that they are enacting a scene of domestic violence that they have witnessed. Nonetheless, without jumping to conclusions, the safeguarding therapist should be alert to all communications. When a child has come to the session with an unexplained bruise on their cheekbone and they are painting two volcanoes, one exploding and one dormant, the therapist should not only be wondering with the child about how to understand what they are bringing, they should also consider thinking things through with relevant school staff to afford the greatest possible insight into the child's home circumstances. Safeguarding is the minefield in the consulting room, so how do we start to make sense of where the school therapist situates themselves in relation to safeguarding practice?

Definitions

The government guide to inter-agency working to safeguard and promote the welfare of children, *Working Together to Safeguard Children* (DfE, 2006/2015) defines safeguarding as: (i) protecting children from maltreatment, (ii) preventing impairment of children's health or development, (iii) ensuring that children grow up in circumstances consistent with the provision of safe and effective care and (iv) taking action to enable all children to have the best outcomes. Everyone who works in a school is charged with the responsibility for promoting wellbeing, and psychotherapists are particularly in the front line, but where we situate ourselves in relation to safeguarding children is less well articulated.

There are four basic categories of child abuse; emotional, physical, sexual, and neglect. Emotional abuse is arguably the most difficult to assess and deal with. Families are emotional units and for many there are exchanges that take place that are not in the child's best interests. Emotional abuse is often attached to physical abuse and neglect, and is difficult to assert in the absence of either or both. Definitions of abuse vary across the four nations of the UK, but the *Working Together to Safeguard Children* (2015) document for England captures the general principles of all:

> ... the persistent emotional maltreatment of a child such as to cause severe and persistent adverse effects on the child's emotional development. It may involve conveying to a child that they are worthless or unloved, inadequate, or valued only insofar as they meet the needs of another person. It may include not giving the child opportunities to express their views, deliberately silencing them or "making fun" of what they say or how they communicate. It may feature age or developmentally inappropriate expectations being imposed on children. These may include interactions that are beyond a child's developmental capability, as well as overprotection and limitation of exploration and learning, or preventing the child participating in normal social interaction. It may involve seeing or hearing the ill-treatment of another. It may involve serious bullying (including

cyber bullying), causing children frequently to feel frightened or in danger, or the exploitation or corruption of children. Some level of emotional abuse is involved in all types of maltreatment of a child, though it may occur alone. (DfE, 2015, p. 92)

Maybe some therapists will read this definition and find resonance in their own history and perhaps, even, in their parenting and family life. Therapists, after all, are human and compromised. It is in part at least, an attitude of shared struggle in surviving families that allows the therapist to take a moral position, without being moralistic, in reflecting on a case where a child is being subject to more than the ordinary challenges of family life. Therapists can reach out to struggling parents and support them in finding ways forward that are less damaging to themselves and their child. Parent partnership work is a psycho-educational hybrid, but is key to working with a child from a troubled family.

Sound knowledge of law and policy is required for all practitioners working with children and the onus is on them to keep abreast of changes to safeguarding. Currently in England and Wales, section 58 of the Children Act 2004, allows for a parent to employ "reasonable punishment" when disciplining their child, but prevents the defence being used in relation to more serious assault charges. Therefore a child disclosing that they had been smacked on the back of their legs for a wrongdoing would not necessarily activate a safeguarding response from a counsellor but might well be greeted with a concerned exploration of the child's feelings around the incident. If a child had been slapped across the face, then this should generate a different response whereby the counsellor and the school might need a closer on-going vigilance about the child's emotional wellbeing. Where on the body, with what force, and the number of times a child is hit are all pieces of information that the therapist needs to understand in order to assess the level of safeguarding concern and therefore it is helpful to enquire into the detail of any upset a child might bring. In *Working Together to Safeguard Children* (2015) physical abuse is defined as:

A form of abuse which may involve hitting, shaking, throwing, poisoning, burning or scalding, drowning, suffocating or otherwise causing physical harm to a child. Physical harm may also be caused when a parent or carer fabricates the symptoms of, or deliberately induces, illness in a child. (DfE, 2015, p. 92)

Physical abuse is the most clear-cut and if a child discloses they have been struck and there is a visible mark, most school staff are confident about their response and the protocols to follow as there is concrete "evidence" to work with. Physical abuse does not need to be persistent to merit attention in the same way that emotional abuse and neglect need to be to activate safeguarding procedures. Further, there is clear statutory guidance on the matter and that is, if the hitting or shaking has left a mark then it needs to be reported to Social Care. It also appears to be more straightforward for children to identify and talk about. In turn, this makes it easier for the therapist to participate in the safeguarding matrix as the rules of engagement are defined.

Neglect, however, is much more difficult to act upon for a number of reasons. *Working Together to Safeguard Children* (2015) defines neglect as:

> The persistent failure to meet a child's basic physical and/or psychological needs, likely to result in the serious impairment of the child's health or development. Neglect may occur during pregnancy as a result of maternal substance abuse. Once a child is born, neglect may involve a parent or carer failing to: i) provide adequate food, clothing and shelter (including exclusion from home or abandonment); ii) protect a child from physical and emotional harm or danger; iii) ensure adequate supervision (including the use of inadequate care-givers); or iv) ensure access to appropriate medical care or treatment. (DfE, 2015, p. 93)

When you are a therapist working in a school in an area of significant social deprivation the definition of neglect might need to be considered within a more political context. Some families exist in severely straightened circumstances where, at times, they can struggle to provide adequate food, clothing, and shelter for their children. Sometimes this is not of their own doing. Some of the more socially isolated parents might struggle to provide adequate supervision for their children and it does not necessarily mean that they are a poor parent or neglectful. This is not to say that these shortfalls in caring for a child can be excused, more than the sources of the failure to meet the needs of the child cannot lie exclusively at the feet of the parent even when the problems are persistent. For example Sonia had previously been in receipt of state benefits but she had to return to work otherwise her benefit payments would have been stopped. Her job as a cleaner meant she had to leave home before the start of school. Sonia had no one she could ask to bring her seven-year-old-son to school, so he had to walk on his own. School found out and were in a position to provide "a walking bus" for the child, but not all schools can be so responsive.

The situation with a seven-year-old walking to school alone on a sustained basis would, in most cases, fall under the rubric of neglect but Sonia might argue that she was in a no-win-situation, that is, if she did not go to work she would be without money to pay for food, so either way her child would suffer. It is not necessarily the case that behind every neglected child there is a neglectful parent, more likely, behind every neglected child there is a struggling parent. The better positioned the therapist is to understand the political and economic circumstances of the family, the better placed the therapist is to untangle the emotional and physical environment of that child.

Perhaps the most emotionally charged aspect of child abuse is when the abuse is sexual. It is not the therapist's job to root out safeguarding concerns, but a therapist needs to be receptive to what the child brings and in the instance of a child who has been sexually abused this is not as straightforward as it might first appear. In *Working Together to Safeguard Children* (2015) sexual abuse is defined as follows:

> … forcing or enticing a child or young person to take part in sexual activities, not necessarily involving a high level of violence, whether or not the child is aware of what is happening. The activities may involve physical contact, including assault by penetration (for example, rape or oral sex) or non-penetrative acts such as masturbation, kissing, rubbing and touching outside of clothing. They may also include non-contact activities, such as involving children in looking at, or in the production of, sexual images, watching sexual activities, encouraging children to behave in sexually inappropriate ways, or grooming a child in preparation for abuse (including via the internet). Sexual abuse is not solely perpetrated by adult males. Women can also commit acts of sexual abuse, as can other children. (DfE, 2015, p. 93)

When a child comes to therapy after a disclosure of sexual abuse, the therapist needs to have a particularly sensitive level of engagement. Even experienced therapists can feel very anxious when working with sexual abuse particularly as it has often taken place between an adult and a child alone together in a room. One of the dynamics involved in sexual abuse is an abuse of power and authority, and two of the myriad feeling states evoked by sexual abuse are fear and acute anxiety. One therapist spoke of her first session with a child recounting that when she shut the door of the therapy room and turned to see the child filled with dread. She immediately opened the door and the door remained ajar until several sessions in when the child closed the door herself.

When children are referred in the immediate aftermath of a disclosure, this might be a challenge for the therapist, particularly with younger children who may not be able to differentiate between a psychotherapist and a social worker for instance. The therapist may get mixed up in the mind of the child with other authorities that are involved, including the police. The child may have been removed from their home or will be in the process of being assessed to be removed. For the child, everything will be up in the air and they may be little interested in either trusting or talking to another stranger. Some therapists feel that because a young child cannot fully contract to a relationship with a therapist there is an uncomfortable replaying of a power dynamic that was part of the abuse. The therapist might need reassuring that benign relationships between adults and children are part of the healing process.

When working with a child who has been subject to sexual abuse, seemingly benign play activity, like the child diving under some cushions and asking the therapist to come and find them, can be unsettling and laden with meaning that feels acutely uncomfortable for the therapist. The transference and countertransference with some children who have been sexually abused can seem like everything is contaminated, nothing is as it seems and all that went before, that could be assumed and trusted, no longer can be. With children who are known to have been sexually abused, over time the psychotherapist may find themselves in the position of receiving a fuller and more detailed picture of the child's experience. It is not so unusual for the child to be removed from the school and therefore therapy is brought prematurely to an end, leaving the child and the therapist with a lot of feelings that are not always possible to fully work through.

It is important, in amongst the emotional turmoil of the unthinkable happening, that there is a thinking beginning to the therapy. The therapist needs to try to clarify their role with the child, as distinct from all the other professionals involved. They also might talk about the possibility that their time together might come to an end quite quickly. For some children it might suit them to talk a little and then leave "it" behind but for many the abuse experience is just too raw to bring, the world too uncertain. The therapist can support the child to make decisions about how to use the space and whether they want to have the space at all at this point in time. Further, it is advisable that counsellors and psychotherapists leave a professional trace with Social Care, that is, ensuring that contact details for the foreseeable future are part of the child's statutory records. There may be insights, albeit briefly, that the therapist has gleaned from their work with the child, and these may be valuable to the child at some point in the future.

Sometimes the therapist will work with a young child who has been groomed to sexually abuse other children and this throws up particular issues for the therapist in relation to confidentiality. The therapist is creating a safe space to talk which then, on some level, could be experienced by the child as an unsafe space which, in effect, opens up into a police interview room when the client discloses that he or she has engaged in sexually abusive behaviours against a younger sibling. Children in this situation often feel unable to talk directly of their experiences. For example, eight-year-old Callum was referred for psychotherapy, and it was known that Callum had been both abused and was, in turn, abusing his younger siblings. In therapy, at first, Callum could not talk about the abuse but his play "talked about" power, sadism, hurting, and watching. Even when Callum did start to open up, the therapist found it quite unbearable to listen to Callum's account, it was easier to see Callum as a victim rather than hearing about his perpetrations. In one session Callum told the therapist that he had heard that children who were abused went on to abuse other people. The therapist told Callum that this was not always the case. Later, the therapist's supervisor pointed out that Callum may be trying to talk about profound worries about his future, and the therapist could not seem to bear to engage with the conversation. Whilst it was indeed the case that not all those who have been abused go on to be abusers, it might well have been helpful for Callum to talk further.

Therapists who work in schools with significant levels of deprivation and therefore overwhelming demands on services, will not be surprised to find that they are managing some difficult emotional transactions between siblings in a school counselling setting in the aftermath of disclosures of sexual abuse. Therapists have found themselves being the only one thinking about a family who Social Care have had to split up due to sexual abuse. We might think, surely, the social worker has organised an opportunity for all the siblings to be gathered before they

part but sometimes social workers are not afforded these opportunities as they are so taken up with finding multiple placements for the
children. In these circumstances therapists need to work closely with
social workers to afford the best endings for the children. Again, this
concerns pulling psychotherapy away from the periphery and into the
thick and think of essential services.

Prevalence, integrated practice, and assessment

All in all working as an integrated safeguarding practitioner throws up
a lot of challenges for the school psychotherapist and it can feel as if it
pulls us out of shape at times. There are just over 13 million children
living in the UK presently, just over 4 million of these are in nursery and
primary school. According to the NSPCC there were 57,000 children
in the UK who were identified as needing protection from abuse in
2015 and they estimate that for every child identified as needing protection from abuse another eight are suffering abuse (Child Protection
Register and Plan, Statistics for all UK nations, NSPCC, 2015). Over
3,000 children were identified as needing protection from sexual abuse.
Thirteen per cent of contacts to the NSPCC helpline in 2015 were concerns about sexual abuse and there were over 47,000 sexual offences
against children (Bentley, O'Hagan, Raff, & Bhatti, 2016). Research has
highlighted that children between the ages of seven and thirteen are
the most vulnerable to sexual abuse (Finkelhor, 1994), with twenty per
cent of children being sexually abused before the age of eight (Snyder,
2000) with a median age of reported abuse at nine years old (Putnam,
2003). Deaf and disabled children are over three times more likely to be
abused than non-deaf and non-disabled children (Jones, et al., 2012).

Some of these children will present with inchoate or substantive
mental health problems and the most recent statistics are that one in ten
children are believed to have a mental health problem yet seventy per
cent of them have not had appropriate interventions at a sufficiently
early age (Mental Health Foundation, 2015). These children might be
referred to Child and Adolescent Mental Health Services (CAMHS),
but an increasing number are seen in school-based services. Many of
us who currently work in schools are of a mind that the vertiginous
thresholds of Social Care mean that the scale of children whose mental wellbeing is under threat is far greater than these statistics suggest. While child deaths from homicide and assault are in long-term
decline, reports of sexual offences against children are increasing, as are

the numbers of children within the child protection system (Bentley, O'Hagan, Raff, & Bhatti, 2016).

Therapists need to be alert to the prevalence of abuse in order to avoid being part of a system that denies the reality of some children's lives. The NSPCC tells us that one in twenty children have been sexually abused and that one in fourteen have been physically abused, one in ten have experienced neglect and that emotional abuse is the second most common reason for children needing protection from abuse (Radford, et al., 2011). This would translate, on average, to at least a number of children in every classroom across the country in need of significant support. As such sensitivity to safeguarding needs to be an integral part of the initial assessment of a new referral.

Many counselling organisations use the Strengths and Difficulties Questionnaire (SDQ) as a matter of routine. We recommend that questions that address safeguarding are also a routine part of assessment when engaging with parents. In our experience, asking if there has been any history of abuse or neglect in the broader family is not experienced as accusatory, rather it gives the parent the space to reflect on their wider family system, and also their family across generations. As blended families are so widespread this question can be a good way of capturing stories and histories across several families. The therapist can prepare the parent to expect some questions asked over the course of the assessment that might be difficult to talk about, and that they can make a choice about what they choose to share. The therapist can also assure parents these questions are asked as a matter of routine in the assessment process, and that they do not have to answer any questions they do not wish to. In our experience no parent has taken issue with such questions and many are relieved to be given a space to respond, sometimes for the first time. If a therapist who is starting out in the work does not feel able to ask such questions then we would recommend, at the close of the assessment, asking a more generic question such as, "Is there anything you think I need to know about your child or the broader family which will help me to better understand and work with your child?" Not asking difficult questions might be safer for the therapist but not safer for the child.

Statutory infrastructure of safeguarding children

The protection of children is enshrined in law, and the school psychotherapist needs to be cognisant of both the spirit and the letter of the law. The Children Act 1989 requires local authorities to give due regard to a child's wishes when determining what services to provide under section 17 of the Children Act 1989, and before making decisions about action to be taken to protect individual children under section 47 of the Children Act 1989. These duties complement requirements relating to the wishes and feelings of children who are, or may be, looked after (section 22 (4) Children Act 1989), including those who are provided with accommodation under section 20 of the Children Act 1989 and children taken into police protection (section 46 (3) (d) of that Act).

The Equality Act 2010 makes public authorities, such as local education authorities, responsible and accountable for maintaining due regard for the need to eliminate discrimination and promote equality of opportunity, and this applies to the process of identification of need and risk faced by children. That is to say, no child or group of children must be treated any less favorably than others in being able to access effective services which meet their particular needs. So for instance the school psychotherapist is able to advocate and even require local authorities to meet the needs of children who might otherwise not be able to easily access psychotherapy, for instance a child with special educational needs and disability. The provision of equitable working spaces and equipment would be another domain where the Equality Act 2010 could be used as leverage to increase resources.

The United Nations Convention on the Rights of the Child (UNCRC) is an international agreement that protects the rights of children and provides a child-centred framework for the development of services to children. The UK Government ratified the UNCRC in 1991 and, by doing so, recognised children's rights to expression and receiving information. Again, the school psychotherapist is able to advocate on behalf of their client and the parents of the child, based on the premise of the UNCRC. The school psychotherapist needs to hold on to the concept that they are part of a safeguarding fabric that is enshrined in law, and that by keeping a second eye on legal frameworks, the psychotherapist can make bureaucracy work for them and their clients in terms of resource building, service provision, and commissioning. It remains to be seen the impact of Brexit on children's rights as so much of what protects children in the UK hails from European directives.

Working together—the safeguarding matrix

The context of safeguarding can be further seen as the range of institutions and stakeholders who together form what we might call the "safeguarding matrix". The psychotherapist needs to hold-in-mind the social and cultural network of the child's world, so alongside the life of the local community, the school itself and the context of the family, the psychotherapist needs to be alert to other professionals who might be involved in the child's life. The psychotherapist needs to gather together a comprehensive picture of a child's world. Schools are situated in communities. These communities are a source of valuable information. Sometimes concerned neighbours and parents will contact a school with information about a child. Staff who work in the school and live in the local community may also have extra awareness about issues that affect the children. When this information pertains to safeguarding, the designated safeguarding person (DSP) needs to make a decision about what to do with this information. Of course, we need to be cautious about hearsay but there have been numerous serious case reviews (Nigel Leat for example) where uneasy feelings reported by staff and parents were not acted upon and children continued to be subject to damaging experiences.

The school psychotherapist is in a position to be able to make connections and safeguarding judgements in relation to the material the child is sharing with them in the sessions. As a picture builds, the immediate safeguarding matrix might extend their enquiry and invite in, say, a school nurse, if there are concerns about neglect. For example, Jess, nine years old, was found to be stealing food from the packed lunches of other children. She was of sufficient concern to be referred to the school psychotherapist. As well as starting sessions, the psychotherapist suggested that the school nurse monitor Jess's weight, paying particular attention to holidays and any weight fluctuations in the absence or presence of school dinners. In one session Jess disclosed that she had been sent to bed without tea the previous evening and had not been given breakfast the following morning. In discussion with the Designated Safeguarding Person (DSP), Social Care were informed of Jess's circumstances. Social Care suggested a Common Assessment Framework (CAF) meeting, and the first of three meetings were arranged. Jess's mother attended these meetings along with Jess's class teacher. The school psychotherapist also attended the meeting and was able to provide an overview of the progress that Jess was making with her. As a result of the CAF meeting, a family support worker was assigned to the family and was able to offer support to Jess's mother, looking at the practical aspects of parenting and household management. The school psychotherapist also offered consultation sessions to Jess's mother. What became apparent was that Jess's mother had experienced a significant degree of neglect herself when she was growing up, and it was possible to draw attention to the way in which history seemed to be replaying itself. Finally, Jess's teacher, now equipped with a fuller picture of Jess's family circumstances, was better able to tailor her expectations to accommodate Jess's developmental difficulties, thereby providing extra support.

We can see from the sequence of events, from Jess stealing food from other children, there followed a collective process whereby a number of practitioners worked together to form a safeguarding matrix. We think it is important to situate therapy within this matrix and much of the steer of policy over recent years has sought to ensure that there are joined up professional systems which protect the child. In this sense, formal therapy should not be seen as something which takes place in a bubble, so to speak. We find ourselves at odds with some colleagues such as Geldard and Geldard (2012) who state that; "Right at the start of therapy we tell the child that what they say to us will be private" (p. 13). The term "private" is problematic and seems to set an unhelpful tone for practice. In light of the post-Laming era where professionals working with children are directed to be more engaged in joined up ways of working, the idea of a "private" conversation tilts towards an outdated insular model of counselling and psychotherapy which leads towards a cul-de-sac of practice axioms which not only undermines the progress and effectiveness of therapy, but also sells short the central contribution that psychotherapists can make in delivering joined up services.

The contemporary culture of counselling and psychotherapy in schools can be traced to the *Every Child Matters* (ECM) (DfE, 2003) initiative, launched in 2003 by the Labour government in response to the Victoria Climbie tragedy. The guidelines had the ambition for "every child to fulfil their potential" and promoted joined up thinking, holistic practice and interagency liaison with particular regard to safeguarding vulnerable children. However the ECM document was not ratified by the coalition government post the 2009 election, and the agenda set by ECM began to drop out of circulation. The term "Every Child Matters" was replaced with the term, "Helping Children Achieve More". The emphasis moved from children mattering to what they could achieve. It was an ideological shift that also saw the dissolution of the Department for Children Schools and Families (DFCSF) which was replaced by the Department for Education (DfE), a shift which appeared to remove the task of children's education from the social fabric.

The Future in Mind (DoH, 2015) is a National Health Service report which offered guidance on how to take mental health services forward for children and young people and the report positioned school counselling as integral to better mental health in schools. The report also outlines ways in which teachers could be supported in increasing their awareness of mental health issues in children. *Mental Health and Behaviour in Schools* (DfE, 2014), alongside *Working Together to Safeguard Children* (DfE, 2015) offered further steer on the challenge of mental wellbeing in schools. Teachers are not only expected to produce impressive academic results but they also have to operate as primary mental health practitioners and safeguarders. In this joined up system of shared responsibilities, the school psychotherapist can no longer work in isolation in the privacy of the therapy room whilst their school colleagues battle on the frontline. Psychotherapy as a politically mute psychic retreat can no longer be defended.

Context

Some therapists working in schools are not always based in the school itself, but rather they drop-in to deliver therapy and therefore have limited contact with school staff. The therapist will have a liaison contact, perhaps with a school nurse or the special education needs and disability coordinator (SENDCO), but the therapist might arrive to see their clients and will only see the school receptionist, who will arrange for the client to come to the session. Therapists who work in this way across schools seem to have something of a nomadic existence and they face different challenges compared to those psychotherapists who are integral to the school, that is, they have a dedicated office and a permanent therapy room kitted out with much of the material they require for therapy. Nonetheless, these nomadic therapists need to find a way of knitting themselves into the safeguarding matrix. The in situ psychotherapist, who will get to know the DSP in the school as part and parcel of being around in the school environs, in meetings and informal spaces like the staff room, while the peripatetic therapist may need to work harder to establish lines of communication and a routine for reporting any concerns. Peripatetic therapists are outsiders and if they are at odds with the school as to how safeguarding matters should progress they might not have the same powers of persuasion as that of an in situ therapist. This could result in the therapist having to pursue the matter independently, thus potentially alienating themselves from the school and the parents. This, in turn, might then jeopardise their continuing relationship with the very child they are trying to protect.

The in situ psychotherapist in the primary school is, potentially, able to get to know all of the children, particularly if there is an informal space where children can bring their worries and have a brief conversation, for instance a lunchtime drop-in service. The model of "drop-in" space takes place at the threshold of formal psychotherapy, and is akin to a mini therapeutic community event (see Chapter One). During the drop-in session the psychotherapist might begin to identify children who otherwise are not registering with teaching staff as overly concerning. A drop-in session can accommodate children who are quietly struggling and who otherwise might get overshadowed by children who are noisier in their presentation. Children can come together, two, three, and sometimes four at a time. At a recent drop-in a child talked about her parents arguing and then fighting at home and as a result of the fight the child had sustained bruising. The accompanying child then said that her mother was often asleep during the day and that she was not getting dressed or cooking tea, but then she was pacing throughout the night. Both these examples constituted safeguarding concerns and the psychotherapist notified the DSP.

Children are a great source of safeguarding for other children and themselves. They are "informants" and if they trust their school, they will bring incidents from outside that have troubled their conscience or hurt their hearts. They will breathe a word of them across the moral barometer that governs within the school and check its reading. And when the reading is out of kilter with the outside, it is they who have to dance the divide, perhaps have to grapple with the feeling that school might demonstrate greater concern than their parent, or their neighbourhood. Children, on the whole, adapt to their environment. They read the rules of home, estate, park, and school and they accommodate each differently. But schools represent the government, the state, and they model the official version of how humans should behave. It is this version that forms the basis of children's social learning and it is schools who have a duty to respond compassionately to the children in their care.

Enquiring into what seems to be safeguarding incidents can leave the therapist navigating the task of interest in the child's safety and well-being whilst being careful not to ask leading questions which might shape the child's responses. The current statutory advice is that it is acceptable to ask for clarification to assist a clearer understanding of what the child is bringing to you. However, the psychotherapist needs to remain sensitive to the fact that if the safeguarding results in a social care intervention the child might be questioned by a number of professionals. Some therapists might worry that questioning a child might be experienced by them as invasive, however in the NSPCC report (2013), *No-one Noticed, No-one Heard; A Study of Disclosures of Childhood Abuse,* retrospective analysis of cases highlighted catalogues of missed opportunities for earlier intervention. The NSPCC report underlined the necessity for professionals to enquire when they feel something is amiss in a child's life. The therapist's curiosity, far from being experienced by the child as intrusive, is more often than not a relief. The NSPCC's more recent report, *It Turned Out Someone Did Care* (2016) details the important role of professionals taking note of the plight of vulnerable children. Ultimately, it could be argued that for the school psychotherapist, it is a matter of positioning oneself between indifference and zeal without ever nearing either.

Perspectives on abuse

The safest place for a child is in school, but some schools have been anything but safe. Child sexual abuse, historically, has featured an institutional dimension and the four nations of the UK have all interrogated institutional abuses since the mid 1980s with various inquiries which make for very uncomfortable reading indeed. Every now and then we are reminded that schools and residential units are not always safe all the time for some children. The Soham murders, where the school site manager murdered two nine-year-old girls from the school, have been burnt into the cultural psyche and activated an overhaul of safeguarding in schools and the creation of the Independent Safeguarding Authority (ISA) where all professional concerns about those who pose a threat to children were logged. This system did not survive into the coalition government and even today concerned professionals are excluded from information systems which might facilitate safe practice. It will be interesting to see how the academisation of failing schools operates safeguarding with its corporate sensibilities which assert data protection over transparency and information sharing. And just as school psychotherapists are finding their feet in terms of becoming core safeguarding professionals and benign arms of the state already the privatisation of child protection has been mooted as the government is looking to enable councils to opt-out of a raft of legal duties toward vulnerable children with the threat of for-profit providers being allowed to take over core child protection functions.

The case in North Somerset, where a primary school teacher Nigel Leat abused children between 2006 and 2011, illustrates just how vulnerable children can be even in the institutions set up to educate and protect them. The North Somerset school involved did not employ a school therapist and you might wonder if the presence of a school psychotherapist would have activated a closer exposition of concerns? It is arguable that a school, or any organisation for that matter, that is serious about safeguarding will commission the consciousness raising capabilities of a psychotherapist (Winship, 2005). It is of note that the Deputy in the school noticed Leat's overly tactile behaviour with the girls. Staff and parents had worries regarding Leat but it took five years for these to reach critical mass. Why does abuse take so long to be outed? The NSPCC (2013) states that the average length between exposure to abuse and disclosure is 7.8 years. But in our experience children will report abuse earlier if people are willing to hear what is being said. Thinking the unthinkable is what therapists sometimes have to do.

Children will disclose to school staff, particularly to TAs who are more able to offer one-to-one time than teachers, but what therapists can offer vulnerable children is unstructured time and a perspective which is trained to listen and look carefully. One of the difficulties that face the therapist is that it is often the most vulnerable children that have parents least likely to consent to begin therapy. So, who are these vulnerable children? Children living with a biological parent and a step-parent are twenty times more likely to be abused than children living with both biological parents (Sedlack, et al., 2010). In our experience, mothers who are unable to identify risk and have struggled to protect themselves from perpetrators of abuse, or weren't protected as children by their mothers, can face great challenges in keeping their own children safe. And this is not to shy away from the fact that women can and do abuse their children.

Working with children where there is a reasonable suspicion that all is not well at home, but no specific disclosures, can be a delicate exchange. Some children work out that the ramifications of a disclosure will significantly disrupt their lives. Action might protect them from an abuser but remove them from a loved but compromised mother, for example. The disclosure also might remove them from their siblings. Some children are so attuned to weighing up bad and badder that by the time they reach a therapist they have a defensive armoury resilient in the face of a gentle enquiry that retreats with the first rebuttal. We can be acutely aware of our responsibilities to safeguard, but children might have a different agenda altogether and that might be the preservation of family at all costs. It is not uncommon for older children to endure abuse and only disclose when they become aware that a younger sibling is looking vulnerable to being abused also. As therapists how do we manage this scenario?

What happens when, for whatever reason, children chose not to avail themselves of this opportunity to disclose abuse to a therapist? Do these children feel as if they have had an opportunity to put a stop to abuse but don't? How do they manage this at the time and subsequently? Bevan, age ten, was a girl from a deeply troubled family where there were significant safeguarding concerns. In therapy she brought her ideal world with an ideal mother. Bevan's insistence that her mother was ideal persisted for months. During one session the therapist said, "You wish for everything to be well and happy in your family but I know there are days when your mum struggles to get you to school, struggles to shop for your lunch, struggles to tell worrying people to leave your home. My guess is that some of these things might trouble you?" Bevan continued with her smile but then later in the session started to talk about a dream in which she was sitting on the top of a high building and there was a glass window between her and her mother. Her siblings were falling from the building and her mother was staring ahead doing nothing. Bevan could not get to her siblings because of the glass window. The dream with its uncomfortable material presented the therapist and Bevan with an opportunity to talk about the more worrying aspects of her life without directly referring to them.

When children talk of their dreams it is almost as if the dream belongs to a hinterland between "of me" and "not of me". In these dreams we come to understand their unconscious but how seriously do we take the unconscious when it comes to safeguarding? How many school therapists have written out a safeguarding form based on a dream and if they did how well received were these by the DSP? And yet we know whilst the unconscious might speak in tangled tongues, it tells the truth. In Bevan's case, the safeguarding concerns reached critical mass and

Social Care processes were initiated. The process of therapy set in place a safeguarding sensibility and when Bevan got to secondary school she did make a disclosure. Along with a steady stream of safeguarding concerns recorded by the therapist and other school staff, gave Social Care the necessary grounds to remove the children from home. When the children were securely placed in foster families further disclosures were made.

Confidentiality as a defence against working together and knowing

There are still some therapists who think it is not appropriate to read a client's history before starting work with them for fear of this interfering with how they meet and work with that client. Personally, we would not want to enter into a room with a client without knowing as full history as possible, not least because it is good practice to safeguard both the client and therapist. If there is a history of violence or particular triggers, then the therapist is better to know about them. Some schools of thought advocate not bringing any extraneous information into the session, arguing that the therapist should wait for the client to bring what they will. We say that it is rather a question of timing. The therapist who works in situ in the school is very much part of the child's working week and will have access to information about that child from several sources. Now, if the child does not bring any of the issues you have been made aware of, say, by a teacher or other children, what does the therapist do? It is part of the therapist's job to work toward psychological integrity and so if there are clear splits between what the child brings to therapy and the therapist's knowledge of what has been happening, then this is an opportunity to heal a split. For instance, in a session seven-year-old Jade told her therapist that "everything is great". But the therapist had been told by Jade's teacher that she had been isolated and quiet all week. So the therapist said; "but Miss Smith told me that you had been struggling this week?" Jade did not seemingly respond and continued with her play in the doll's house where baby was in the loft and mummy was in the kitchen. A short time later the baby and mummy were reunited.

Fluidity between inside the session and outside is a necessary ingredient of good practice. In Jade's case it was helpful for her to know that her teacher shared her concerns with the therapist, and that there is in turn a continuity flowing in the other direction, that is to say, the container of concern about wellbeing extends beyond the parameter of the therapy room. The therapeutic space is not hermetically sealed in a school, and nor should it be. The school safeguarding matrix should feel like a containing and safe space, where even the walls feel safe; a "Brick Mother" to borrow a phrase from Henri Rey.

Generally, who attends the counselling service is the worst kept secret in a school with often the therapist being the only person not to openly acknowledge who they are seeing. We would argue for a much greater degree of transparency regarding who is in receipt of counselling in a school. What message are we sending out if we try to secrete the child in and out of the classroom on their way to and from therapy? That would seem only to increase the sense that it is shameful to be in receipt of therapy. Children attending a school counselling service can experience themselves as part of a beleaguered but privileged reconstituted family. At the point of "contracting" with a child the therapist can ask the child what they need from the service in terms of confidentiality and if they never want you to breath a word that they are using the service in a school, you are going to have to unearth an invisible cloak.

Confidentiality often seems to be an issue for children who have something to hide, typically attached to worries that they might be taken from their parents, however for most young children confidentiality is not uppermost in their minds and this is not because they are not able to think through the ramifications fully. In fact most children come to therapy because in one way or another they exist in a state of dislocation when they need to exist in a state of connectedness to a benign, holding matrix of concern. Further, not being able to tell might very well be the reason some children are in counselling in the first place. Jack, aged eight, who came from a family with safeguarding concerns and was familiar with how the safeguarding systems in the school operated, spent most of one session remonstrating with his therapist about how he wanted to tell her something, but she was "not to tell anyone else". The therapist said she could not offer Jack the reassurance he needed, that if it was something which made her worry that he might not be safe she would have to tell the head teacher. Jack remonstrated with her further until he finally gave up his secret, that he did not love his dad and what was going to happen now? Jack was worried that he might leave him when he found out. The therapist spoke to him about how love kept us safe and when it was not there we felt more fragile in the world. She wondered with him why he might not love his dad and said that what he had said was important but, on this occasion, she did not think she needed to pass this on to anyone else.

When Jack discovered over the next few weeks that nothing catastrophic had happened, it was helpful for him to know that putting things into words, especially the things that worried him, did not bring his world crashing down around him. This exchange reminded the therapist that children having to navigate what information does and doesn't leave the therapy room is not at all straightforward for Jack put previous safeguarding incidents into a different hierarchy in terms of pain and worry. Actually most young children assume that adults will talk to one another about them, and they seem naturally disinclined to have concerns about confidentiality between adults. It is adults and perhaps the psychotherapy profession in particular, that is overly preoccupied with the matter.

Safe and unsafe practice—a note on touching words

That all therapy rooms need a viewing panel should go without saying but beyond that how do therapists keep themselves and the child safe? Children are often more tactile than adults. They might wrap their arms around their counsellor when they see them in the school. To recoil from this would be hurtful but the more in tune the therapist is with the child, the less there is need for touch as expression. Our advice would be always to notice and to try and find the words to express the sentiment and emotion behind a moment of physical contact; for example, the therapist might say; "I think you have missed me, so you want to hold my hand?" As described earlier, this interpretive technique seeks to find words to speak as loud as actions. Some children hold onto their therapist as if they are the last lifeboat, some "attack" with a hug, burying themselves as if trying to climb inside some imagined marsupial space. A therapist should not instigate touch but rather we like Ferguson's (2011) idea of practitioner's building up their resilience to touch and intimacy when working with young clients. Receiving physical contact might be a part of the early therapeutic relationship and an essential communication which the therapist needs to relate to.

But touch can mean different things for different children. Working with children who have been sexually abused opens up a different set of concerns if the child makes physical contact with the therapist. Operating a no-touch policy may be a safeguarding ideal, but in practice it is impossible and might risk missing some of the child's desperate non-verbal communication. Better to operate a practice policy of interpreting touch, that is to say, finding words to communicate the meaning behind the physical contact. Experience points towards a diminution in touch when it has been verbalised and understood. Of course, there are gender differentials and male therapists have to be more keenly aware of the meaning of touch, and work towards words replacing actions.

When working with children of primary school age there is something specific about the basic biological needs that they present in a session. For instance if you have a young client who comes to a session at nine in the morning saying that they feel sick and you discover that they have not eaten since lunchtime yesterday, then your first intervention might be to make some toast for them. Some children may have experienced significant disruption in sleep, so coming to a session and falling asleep might be a strong biological urge and not a defensive manoeuvre. Sometimes hunger and sleepiness are a priority and the therapist should accommodate these states. Of course a child falling asleep in a session might place both the therapist and the child in a vulnerable position for whilst a client isn't awake in the presence of another there is an imbalance.

To merely interpret a child's need to go to the toilet might result in a messy outcome if a toilet break is not accommodated. But flatulence can be a valuable communication from the bowels of the child filling the room and indeed our nostrils with a bad smell, waste, the churning movement of psychic disequilibrium making its presence smelt, so to speak. Fear can often be expressed through the bowels, in fact in colloquial expression the two are clearly associated. So how does the therapist receive descriptive language that might receive a detention if used outside of the therapy room? We might say that crudeness is not admonished but the aim is to understand what it means to use a word that is otherwise taboo.

The future

In spite of the tributaries of contemporary safeguarding practice reaching back to a genuine advocacy of children's welfare, whenever human systems respond there is a by-product and the by-product in this case is blame. We know what happens when safeguarding goes wrong. The high profile cases of Victoria Climbie and Baby P and the fate of various employees of Haringey Social Services can attest to the vilification of those who work with vulnerable children. School Counselling Services and all professionals working with children live in fear of a child dying on their watch. Mechanisms can turn the responsibilities of safeguarding into "covering one's back". Once a safeguarding form has been filled out and the responsibility passed on then the professional does not have to think about it. If there are organisations which are punitive to staff who might have missed an expression of vulnerability in a family then there might be an incentive to conceal a future "miss". This does not help keep children safe.

Is it necessary to execute a paradigm shift where parents do not "own" the emotional health of their children, just as they feel they don't have exclusive responsibility to educate their children? Would Daniel Pelka have died of starvation and Shanay Walker of abuse, in front of the concerned eyes of a school, if deference to the parent's and carer's authority didn't override active compassion? And by active compassion we mean taking concerns and curiosity and doing something with them. The onus should be removed from parents to feel they are the sole providers of emotional nurture for their children rather children "own" it themselves and can take responsibility for it. Within this "new" paradigm school counselling services would not require parental permission to see a child if the child referred themselves. How many school therapists have been petitioned repeatedly by children where they suspect something at home is "not right" and yet without parental permission they can only refuse them gently. On some level are they relieved? How many therapists remember when that same child who begged and begged to come to see you simply gave up and stopped trying? How many therapists can still recall that child's empty gaze as they read this?

There is an unfolding complex picture when it comes to the growing number of cultural factors to consider when safeguarding children (Phoenix & Hussain, 2007). In the UK we need to be more research interested in race, culture, and how this impacts on bringing up and safeguarding children. Neil Garnham QC who resided over the Laming Inquiry, one of our most defining failures of child protection, involving Victoria Climbie, said in 2003;

> Assumptions based on race can be just as corrosive in its effect as
> blatant racism … racism can affect the way people conduct them-
> selves in other ways. Fear of being accused of racism can stop people

acting when otherwise they would. Assumptions that people of the same colour, but from different backgrounds, behave in similar ways can distort judgments. (DoH, 2003, p. 15)

In fact, several studies suggest that it is the socioeconomic status that is more divisive and defining than race and that essentialist constructions of race and culture are unhelpful. Ethnic minorities and those from high socioeconomic backgrounds are substantially more likely to go to university than white British pupils and those from the lowest socio-economic backgrounds. Would Daniel Pelka have died if his ethnic category was White UK? Could the school have dug deeper about Daniel's "eating condition"? What about involving the school nurse, contacting the GP? Of course, if the school were fully aware of the life threatening nature of Daniel's situation they would have acted but what we are talking about is the journey toward that knowing. And embarking on that journey feels treacherous, in part, because it feels as if it's violating the parent's ownership of that child and that an adult's word is to be trusted over a child's documentary evidence to the contrary. What's less safe for a child?

So, what are we to make of this emerging but pixelated landscape and where do therapists working in schools place themselves in relation to all of this? Do we need to reframe ourselves away from the private, non-essential, and confidential domain over a safeguarding workforce, essential, transparent, accountable, and public? Will this infrastructure exist as a statutory force in a decade's time or just as we emerge with the blunt trauma of a statistical overview of the abuse of children will it be sequestered into private pockets? It is of note that OFSTED requires every boarding school to have a counsellor in situ but the same requirement is not made of the many schools serving some of the most deprived areas in England where poor children are more likely to be on the child protection register. Parents cannot take the strain alone, nor can struggling social workers. Psychotherapists working in primary school are in a unique and privileged position to both gain insight into the lives of vulnerable children, to theory build, to research, and to make some inroads into democratising opportunity and improving resilience through early intervention and safeguarding. The in situ therapist, working as an integrated practitioner with her teaching and pastoral colleagues in primary schools can make a real contribution to safer tomorrows for children.

REFERENCES

Ainsworth, M. D. S., & Bell, S. M. (1970). Attachment, exploration, and separation: Illustrated by the behavior of one-year-olds in a strange situation. *Child Development*, *41*(1): 49–67.

Ainsworth, M. D. S., Bell, S. M., & Stayton, D. (1974). Infant-mother attachment and social development. In: M. P. Richards (Ed.), *The Introduction of the Child into a Social World* (pp. 99–135). London: Cambridge University Press.

Ainsworth, M. D. S., Blehar, M. C., Waters, E., & Wall, S. (1978). *Patterns of Attachment: A Psychological Study of the Strange Situation*. Hillsdale, NJ: Erlbaum.

Allen, J. G., Fonagy, P., & Bateman, A. (2008). *Mentalizing in Clinical Practice*. Arlington, VA: American Psychiatric Publishing.

Alvarez, A. (2010). Levels of analytic work and levels of pathology: The work of calibration. *The International Journal of Psychoanalysis, 91*: 859–878.

Aron, L. (2006). Analytic impasse and the third: Clinical implications of intersubjectivity theory. *The International Journal of Psychoanalysis, 87*: 349–368.

Atkins, R. N. (1983). Peer relatedness in the first year of life: The birth of a new world. *Annual Psycho-Analysis, 11*: 227–244. New York, NY: International Universities Press.

Balint, M. (1950). Changing therapeutical aims and techniques in psycho-analysis. *International Journal Psycho-Analysis, 31*: 117–122.

Balint, M. (1968). *The Basic Fault*. London: Tavistock.

Bauman, Z. (2001). *Community—Seeking Safety in an Insecure World*. Cambridge: Polity Press.

BBC. (2014). *Frozen* becomes fifth-biggest film in box office history www.bbc.co.uk/news/entertainment-arts-27585310 [Last accessed 28 May 2017].

Bentley, H., O'Hagan, O., Raff, A., & Bhatti, I. (2016). *How Safe are our Children? The Most Comprehensive Overview of Child Protection in the UK*. London: NSPCC.

Bick, E. (1964). Notes on infant observation in psychoanalytical training. *International Journal Psycho-Analysis, 45*: 558–566.

Bick, E. (1968). The function of the skin in early object relations. *International Journal of Psycho-Analysis, 49*: 484–486.

Bion, W. R. (1959). Attacks on linking. *International Journal of Psychoanalysis, 30*: 308–315.

Bion, W. R. (1962). *Learning from Experience*. London: Heinemann.

Bion, W. R. (1967). *Second Thoughts*. London: Maresfield Press, 1987.

Bion, W. R. (1970). *Attention & Interpretation*. London: Karnac, 1993.

Blatz, W. (1940). *Hostages to Peace: Parents and the Children of Democracy*. New York, NY: Morrow.

Bor, R., Ebner-Landy, J., Gill, S., & Brace, C. (2002). *Counselling in Schools*. London: Sage.

Boulton, M. (2005). School peer counselling for bullying services as a source of social support: a study with secondary school pupils. *British Journal of Guidance and Counselling, 33*: 485–494.

Bowlby, J. (1951). Maternal care and mental health. In: *World Health Organization Monograph* (Serial No. 2). Geneva: WHO.

Bowlby, J. M. (1953). *Child Care and the Growth of Love*. Harmondsworth: Pelican.

Bowlby, J. M. (1959). Separation anxiety. *International Journal of Psycho-Analysts, 16*: 1–25.

Bowlby, J. M. (1969). *Attachment and Loss, Vol. 1: Attachment*. London: Hogarth.

Bowlby, J. M. (1973). *Attachment and Loss, Vol. 2: Separation, Anxiety & Anger*. London: Hogarth.

Bowlby, J. M. (1980). *Attachment and Loss, Vol. 3: Loss, Sadness and Depression*. London: Hogarth.

Bowlby, J. M. (1988). *A Secure Base. Parent-Child Attachment and Healthy Human Development*. Routledge: London.

Breuer, J., & Freud, S. (1895). *Studies on Hysteria*. J. Strachey (Trans.). *The Standard Edition of the Complete Psychological Works of Sigmund Freud, Vol. II*. London: Hogarth, 1955.

Briggs, A. (Ed). (2002). *Surviving Space: Papers on Infant Observation*. London: Karnac.

Carter, A. (2015). *Carter Review of Initial Teacher Training*. www.gov.uk/government/uploads/system/uploads/attachment_data/file/399957/Carter_Review.pdf [last accessed 4 May 2017].

Chiesa, M. (1993). At the border between institutionalization and community psychiatry: Psychodynamic observations of a hospital admission ward. *Free Associations, 4*, 2: 241–264.

Chodorow, N. (1978). *The Reproduction of Mothering*. California, CA: University Press.

Danuinaite, D., Cooper, M., & Forster, T. (2015). Counselling in UK primary schools: Outcomes and predictors of change. *Counselling & Psychotherapy Research, 51*: 251–261.

Department for Education. (2015). *Working Together to Safeguard Children*. London: HMSO.

Department for Education. (2003). *Every Child Matters*. London: HMSO.

Department for Education. (2014). *Mental Health & Behaviour in Schools*. London: HMSO.

Department of Health Laming Report. (2003). *The Victoria Climbie Inquiry*. London: HMSO.

Department of Health. (2004). *Children's National Service Framework*. London: HMSO.

Department of Health. (2011). *No Health Without Mental Health*. London: HMSO.

Department of Health. (2014). *Closing the Gap: Priorities for Essential Change in Mental Health*. London. HMSO.

Department of Health. (2015). *Future in Mind—Promoting, Protecting and Improving our Children and Young Peoples Mental Health and Well Being*. London: HMSO.

Diamond, J. (2016). Current therapeutic community work with children and young people. *Therapeutic Communities: The International Journal of Therapeutic Communities, 37*(1): 1–2.

Durlak, J., Weissberg, R. P., Dymnicki, A. B., Taylor, R. D., & Schellinger, K. B. (2011). The impact of enhancing students' social and emotional learning: a meta-analysis of school-based universal interventions. *Child Development, 82*(1): 405–432.

Ecclestone, K., & Hayes, D. (2010). *The Dangerous Rise of Therapeutic Education*. Routledge: London.

Erikson, E. H. (1950). *Childhood and Society*. New York, NY: Norton.

Erikson, E. H. (1968). *Identity: Youth and Crisis*. New York, NY: Norton.

Ferguson, H. (2011). *Child Protection Practice*. London: Palgrave Macmillan.

Finkelhor, D. (1994). Current information on the scope and nature of child sexual abuse. *Sexual Abuse of Children, 4*: 31–53.

Fonagy, P. (1999). The transgenerational transmission of holocaust trauma. *Attachment & Human Development, 1*(1): 92–114.

Freud, A., & Burlingham, D. (1944). *Infants Without Families*. London: Allen and Unwin.

Freud, S. (1900). *The Interpretation of Dreams*. J. Strachey (Trans.). *The Standard Edition of the Complete Psychological Works of Sigmund Freud IV & V*. London: Hogarth, 1955.

Freud, S. (1901). *The Psychopathology of Everyday Life*. Harmondsworth: Penguin, 2003.

Freud, S. (1905). *Wit and its Relation to the Unconscious*. New York, NY: Norton, 1960.

Freud, S. (1910). The future prospects of psycho-analytic therapy. *The Standard Edition of the Complete Psychological Works of Sigmund Freud XI* (pp. 144–145). London: Hogarth, 1955.

Frozen. (2013). C. Buck & J. Lee (Dir.). Burbank, CA: Walt Disney Pictures.

Gardener, D. E. M. (1969). *Susan Isaacs*. London: Methuen Educational.

Geldard, K., & Geldard, D. (2012). *Counselling Children—A Practical Introduction*. London: Sage.

George, C., & Solomon, J. (1996). Representational models of relationships: Links between caregiving and attachment. *Infant Mental Health Journal, 17*: 198–216.

Gulliver, A., Griffiths, K. M., & Christensen, H. (2010). Perceived barriers and facilitators to mental health help-seeking in young people: a systematic review. *BMC Psychiatry, 10*: 113–123.

Hall, C., Hall, E., & Hornby, G. (2002). *Counselling Pupils in Schools, Skills and Strategies for Teachers*. London: Routledge.

Halpern, D. (1995). *Mental Health and the Built Environment*. London: Taylor & Francis.

Harlow, H. (1958). The nature of love. *American Psychologist, 13*: 673–685.

Hartman, A. (1995). Diagrammatic assessment of family relationships. *Families in Society, 76*: 111–121.

HC 342 House of Commons Health Committee. (2014). *Children's and Adolescents' Mental Health and CAMHS. Third Report of Session 2014–2015*. London: Stationary Office.

Heimann, P. (1950). On Counter-transference. *International Journal of Psycho-Analysis, 31*: 81–84.

Hesse, E., Cassidy, J., & Shaver, P. R. (Eds). (2008). The Adult Attachment Interview: Protocol, method of analysis, and empirical studies. In: *Handbook of Attachment: Theory, Research and Clinical Applications, 2nd Ed.*, (pp. 552–598). New York, NY: Guildford Press.

Hinshelwood, R. D. (1989). *A Dictionary of Kleinian Thought*. London: Free Association Books.

Hinshelwood, R. D. (1994a). The relevance of psychotherapy. *Psychoanalytic Psychotherapy, 8*: 283–294.

Hinshelwood, R. D. (1994b). Attacks on reflective space. In: V. L. Schermer & M. M. Pines, (Eds.), *Ring of Fire—Primitive Affects and Object Relations in Group Psychotherapy* (pp. 86–106). London: Routledge.

Hinshelwood, R. D., & Skogstad, W. (Eds). (2000). *Observing Organisations: Anxiety, Defence and Culture in Health Care.* London: Routledge.

Hochchild, A. (1983). *The Managed Heart: Commercialization of Human Feeling.* Berkeley, CA: University of California Press.

Holmes, J. (1993). *John Bowlby and Attachment Theory.* London: Routledge.

Institute for Public Policy Research. (2016). www.mentalhealth.org.uk/a-to-z/c/children-and-young-people. [last accessed 4 May 2017]. IPPR.

Isaacs, S. (1929). *The Nursery Years.* London: Routledge & Kegan Paul.

Isaacs, S. (1933). *Social Development in Young Children.* London: Routledge.

Isaacs, S. (1952). The nature and function of phantasy. In: J. Riviere (Ed.), *Developments in Psychoanalysis* (pp. 67–77). London: Hogarth.

Jackson, E. (2002). Mental health in schools. What about the staff? *Journal of Child Psychotherapy, 28*: 129–146.

Jones, L., Bellis, M. A., Wood, S., Hughes, K., McCoy, E., Eckley, L., & Bates, G. (2012). *Prevalence and Risk of Violence Against Children with Disabilities: A Systematic Review and Meta-analysis of Observational Studies.* Centre for Public Health, Liverpool John Moores, University: Liverpool.

Johnson, J. G., Cohen, P., Kasen, S., Skodol, A. E., Hamagami, F., & Brook, J. S. (2000). Age-related change in personality disorder trait levels between early adolescence and adulthood: a community-based longitudinal investigation. *Acta Psychiatrica Scandinavia, 102*: 265–275.

Kestenberg, J. S. (1982). A metapsychological assessment based on an analysis of a survivor's child. In: M. S. Bergmann, & M. E. Jucovy. (Eds.), *Generations of the Holocaust* (pp. 137–158). New York, NY: Columbia University Press.

Klein, M. (1932). *The Psycho-Analysis of Children.* London: Random House, 1997.

Klein, M. (1946). Notes on some schizoid mechanisms. *International Journal of Psychoanalysis, 27*: 99–110.

Klein, M. (1955). The psychoanalytic play technique. History and significance. In: *Envy & Gratitude—Collected papers, 1946–1963* (pp. 122–141). London: Vintage, 1997.

Klein, M. (1961). *Narrative of a Child Analysis.* London: Hogarth.

Krauss, R. E. (1994). *The Optical Unconscious.* Cambridge, Massachusetts, MA. MIT Press.

Lacan, J. (1960). The subversion of the subject and the dialectic of desire in the freudian unconscious. In: *Ecritis* (pp. 292–324). London: Routledge, 1977.

Laing, R. D. (1984). *Politics of Experience*. Harmondsworth: Penguin.

Liekerman, M. (1995). A debate on child psychoanalysis; Anna Freud and Melanie Klein. In: S. A. Gillman, & Zipes, A. (Eds.), *The Yale Book of Jewish Culture in Germany*. New York, NY: Yale University Press, 1996.

Lines, D. (2002). *Brief Counselling in Schools—Working with 11–18 Year Olds*. London: Sage.

Lyons-Ruth, K. (1996). Attachment relationships among children with aggressive behaviour problems: The role of disorganized early attachment patterns. *Journal of Consulting and Clinical Psychology, 64*: 64–73.

MacDonald, S. (2015). The incubator psyche. *Psychoanalytic Psychotherapy, 9*(1): 88–106.

Mackenzie-Smith, S. (1992). A psychoanalytical observational study of the elderly. *Free Associations, 3*: 355–390.

Main, M., & Hesse, E. (1990). Parents' unresolved traumatic experiences are related to infant disorganized attachment status: Is frightened and/or frightening parental behaviour the linking mechanism? In: M. Greenberg, D. Cicchetti, & E. M. Cummings. (Eds.), *Attachment in the Preschool Years; Theory, Research and Intervention* (pp. 161–182). Chicago: University of Chicago Press.

Main, M., & Solomon, J. (1986). Discovery of a new insecure-disorganized/disoriented attachment pattern. In: M. Yogman & T. B. Brazelton. (Eds.), *Affective Development in Infancy* (pp. 95–124). Norwood, NY: Ablex Press.

Meltzer, D. (1974). Adhesive identification. In: A. Hahn (Ed.), *Sincerity and Other Works: Collected Papers of Donald Meltzer* (pp. 335–350). London: Karnac.

Mental Health Foundation. (2015). *Fundamental Facts About Mental Health*. www.mentalhealth.org.uk/sites/default/files/fundamental-facts-15.pdf [last accessed 4 May 2017].

Miller, L., Rustin, M. E., Rustin, M. J., & Shuttleworth, J. (Eds). (1989). *Closely Observed Infants*. London: Duckworth.

Moloney, J. C. (1954). Mother, God and superego. *Journal of the American Psychoanalytic Association, 2*: 120–151.

Music, G. (2007). Learning our lessons: some issues arising from delivering mental health services in schools. *Psychoanalytic Psychotherapy, 21*(1): 1–19.

National Foundation for Educational Research (NfER). (2016). *Developing School Counselling Services for Children in Wales*. www.nfer.ac.uk/nfer/publications/WPV01/WPV01.pdf [last accessed 4 May 2017].

NSPCC. (2013). *Child Abuse and Neglect in the UK Today*. London: NSPCC.

NSPCC. (2013). *No-one Noticed, No-one Heard; A Study of Disclosures of Childhood Abuse*. London: NSPCC.

NSPCC. (2015). Child Protection Register and Plan, Statistics for all UK nations www.nspcc.org.uk/globalassets/documents/statistics-and-information/child-protection-register-statistics-united-kingdom.pdf [last accessed 15 June 2017].

Office of National Statistics. (2016). *Suicide in the United Kingdom.* Released December 2nd. www.ons.gov.uk/search?q=suicide+2016 [last accessed 15 June 2017].

Ogden, T. H. (2004). The analytic third: implications for psychoanalytic theory and technique. *Psychoanalytic Quarterly, 73*(1): 167–195.

Phillips, L., & Smith, R. (2011). *Developing School Counselling Services for Children and Young People in Wales.* Wales: National Foundation for Education Research.

Phoenix, A., & Hussain, F. (2007). *Parenting and Ethnicity Report.* York: Joseph Rowntree Foundation.

Piaget, J. (1951). *Play, Dreams and Imitation in Childhood.* London: Routledge & Kegan Paul.

Piontelli, A. (1992). *From Foetus to Child.* London: Routledge.

Pious, W. L. (1950). The pathogenic process in schizophrenia. *Psychoanalytic Quarterly, 19*: 282–283.

Place2Be. (2010). *Cost-effective Positive Outcomes for Children and Families: An Economic Analysis of The Place2Be's Integrated School-based Services.* London: Place2Be.

Ploye, P. (2006). *The Prenatal Theme in Psychotherapy.* London: Karnac.

Putnam, F. (2003). Ten-year research update review: Child sexual abuse. *Journal of the American Academy of Child and Adolescent Psychiatry, 42*: 269–278.

Radford, L., Corrall, S., Bradley, C., Fisher, H., Bassett, C., Howart, N., & Collishaw, S. (2011). *Child Abuse and Neglect in the UK Today.* London: NSPCC.

Rey, H. (1994). *Universals of Psychoanalysis in the Treatment of Psychotic and Borderline States. Factors of Space-Time and Language.* London. Free Association Books.

Robertson, J. (1953). *A Two Year Old Goes to Hospital.* New York, NY: New York University Film Library [distributor], 1953.

Rosenfeld, H. (1952). Transference-phenomena and transference-analysis in an acute catatonic schizophrenic patient. *International Journal of Psycho-Analysis, 33*: 457–464.

Rustin, M. (1989). Observing infants: Reflections on methods. In: L. Miller, M. Rustin, M. Rustin, & J. Shuttleworth. (Eds.), *Closely Observed Infants* (pp. 52–78). London: Duckworth.

Rustin, M. (1994). A significant step for infant observation. Report on the infant observation conference, Tavistock, London; 1–4 September 1993. *Newsletter for the Association of Psychoanalytic Psychotherapy, 14*: 6–7.

Rutter, M., Maughan, B., Mortimore, P., Ouston, J., & Smith, A. (1979). *15,000 Hours—Secondary Schooling and their Effects on Children*. London: Paul Chapman, 1994.

Salome, L. A. (1916/1962). The dual-orientation of narcissism. *Psychoanalytic Quarterly*, 31(1–2): 1–30.

Salzberger-Wittenberg, I., Williams, G., & Osborne, E. (1993). *The Emotional Experience of Learning & Teaching*. London: Karnac.

Samuels, Z. (2015). Mental health detentions hit an all-time high. Black Mental Health UK, www.blackmentalhealth.org.uk/index.php/news/news-archive/1649-mental-health-detentions-hit-all-time-high-amid-human-rights-concerns-in-its-use-against-black-britons. [last accessed 3 August 2016].

Sedlak, A. J., Mettenburg, J., Basena, M., Petta, I., McPherson, K., Greene, A., & Li, S. (2010). *Fourth National Incidence Study of Child Abuse and Neglect (NIS–4): Report to Congress*. Washington, DC: US Department of Health and Human Services, Administration for Children and Families.

Segal, H. (1986). *Delusion and Artistic Creativity and other Psychoanalytic Essays*. London: Free Association Books.

Segal, H. (1991). *Dream, Phantasy, Art*. London: Tavistock/Routledge.

Smith, P. (2011). *Emotional Labour of Nurses Revisited*. London: Palgrave.

Snyder, H. N. (2000). *Sexual Assault of Young Children as Reported to Law Enforcement: Victim, Incident, and Offender Characteristics*. Washington, DC: US Department of Justice, Office of Justice Programs, Bureau of Justice Statistics.

Solomon, J. C. (1955). Nail Biting and the integrative process. *International Journal of Psycho-Analysis*, 36: 393–395.

Stern, D. (1985). *The Interpersonal World of the Infant: A View from Psychoanalysis and Developmental Psychology*. New York, NY: Basic Books.

Stern, D. (1995). *The Motherhood Constellation: A Unified View of Parent–Infant Observation*. New York, NY: Basic Books.

Stern, D. (2000). "The relevance of empirical infant research to psychoanalytic theory and practice". In: J. Sandler, & M. Sandler. (Eds.), *Clinical and Observational Psychoanalytic Research: Roots of a Controversy* (pp. 73–90). London: Karnac.

Strachey, J. (1933). The nature of the therapeutic action of psychoanalysis. *International Journal Psycho-Analysis*, 50: 275–292.

Trevarthen, C. (1979). Communication and cooperation in early infancy: a description of primary intersubjectivity. In: M. Bullowa (Ed.), *Development of Communication: Social and Pragmatic Factors in Language Acquisition* (pp. 321–347). London: Wiley.

Tustin, F. (1982). *Austic States in Children*. London: Routledge Kegan & Paul.

Waddell, M. (2013). Infant observation in Britain: a tavistock approach. *Infant Observation: International Journal of Infant Observation and its Applications, 16*(1): 4–22.

Weare, K. (2004). *Developing the Emotionally Literate School.* London: Paul Chapman.

Winnicott, D. W. (1949). Hate in the counter-transference. In: *Through Paediatrics to Psycho-Analysis* (pp. 195–203). London: Hogarth.

Winnicott, D. W. (1951). Transitional objects and transitional phenomena. In: *Collected Papers: Through Paediatrics to Psychoanalysis* (pp. 229–243). London: Tavistock, 1958.

Winnicott, D. W. (1960). The theory of the parent-infant relationship. *International Journal of Psycho-Analysis, 41*: 585–595.

Winship, G. (1995). The unconscious impact of caring for acutely disturbed patients. *Journal of Psychiatric and Mental Health Nursing, 2*: 227–233.

Winship, G. (2001). Notes on the research technique of infant group observation. *Group Analysis, 34*: 245–258.

Winship, G. (2005). Consciousness raising and well-being in public sphere organisations. *Psychoanalytic Psychotherapy, 19*: 233–245.

Winship, G. (2007). The ethics of reflective research in single case study inquiry. *Perspectives in Psychiatric Care, 43*: 174–182.

Winship, G. (2008). Working with staff dynamics in an educational setting: the staff support group that wasn't to be. In: D. Kennard (Ed.), *Staff Support Groups in the Public Sector* (pp. 120–140). London: Wiley.

Winship, G., & Knowles, J. (1997). The transgenerational impact of cultural trauma-linking phenomena in the treatment of third generation survivors of the holocaust. *British Journal of Psychotherapy, 13*: 259–266.

Woodhead, M. (1976). *Intervening in Disadvantage. A Challenge for Nursery Education.* London: National Foundation for Education Research.

Young Minds. (2016). www.youngminds.org.uk/news/blog/2937.

INDEX